What Can I Ask

What Can I Ask
New and Selected Poems 1975–2014

Elana Dykewomon

sapphic classics from
A MIDSUMMER NIGHT'S PRESS
& SINISTER WISDOM

What Can I Ask: New and Selected Poems 1975–2014
by Elana Dykewomon

A Midsummer Night's Press
16 West 36th Street
2nd Floor
New York, NY 10018
amidsummernightspress@gmail.com
www.amidsummernightspress.com

Sinister Wisdom, Inc.
P.O. Box 3252
Berkeley, CA 94703
sinisterwisdom@gmail.com
www.sinisterwisdom.org

Designed by Nieves Guerra.
Cover photo © Cathy Cade. Used with permission.
Sitting above Elana's desk in front of some of her journals are
ceramic figures by Cindy Chan. Chan is a clay artist who sculpts in
Pacifica, California at Clay Creations.

First edition, April 2015

ISBN-13: 978-1-938334-15-3

Simultaneously published as *Sinister Wisdom* 96, ISSN: 0196-1853.

The author extends her thanks to the following journals and
editors where these poems originally appeared: "Butch resisting
the pressure to change gender," *Sojourner*, Boston, April 2000,
"When to Answer," *ZYZZYVA*, Vol. X, No. 2, Summer, 1994.

Printed in the U.S. on recycled paper.

Contents

Preface: *Elana's Garden in Belgrade* by Lepa Mladjenović 11

Introduction: *Rekindle the Spark, Ignite a New Fire* by Jewelle Gomez ... 17

New Poems 23

I have just begun this 25
Women in Black 26
Assignment 27
Pauline Newman at 92 29
Butch resisting the pressure to change gender 33
When to answer 36
Unravel, then 38
California 40
dream fish 41
Now about old women – 42

Nothing Will Be As Sweet As The Taste Selections 43

[If you were my home] 45
she says she is 46
A lesbian's prerogative 47
Knowledge in the Biblical Sense 49

Carnal Knowledge 51
The Census Taker Interviews the 20th Century 53
A Law of Physics 59
fifteen minutes from the kar kare klinic 60
desire, jews, casino 62
big belly on the road from reno 66
poem for my unborn niece 72
the real fat womon poems 73
[only] 83
Some notes on the nature of the bad queen 84
A fool for love 87
oakland: february 1991, 1 a.m 89
Trying to understand Rosebud 91
american wounds 94
Woodpeckers 95
Poem for the protection of my loved ones 98
Take anything 99
These things: 101
A deliberate slowing 102
the thing we long for 103
Blood letting 104
My mother's gifts 106
my mother used to have that dream 107
We change each other 109
Tell me a story 110
Carrying the Ark 112
Alchemy 114
great barrier reef 115
even my eyes become mouths 116
like paradise 117
Bowls—A Series 118
    The Gift 118
    Glass 121
    Wood 123
    Pottery 127
    Metal 129
    Night & Sky 130

fragments from lesbos Selections 133

[Everyone] 135
[Great stars sweep the sky] 136
[Amy] 136
[you don't ask but i] 137
[Highway 99. Every time. 137
[before you are gone] 138
[she walks at sunset along the shore] 139
[give me a wide sky] 139
[let the softness enter you woman] 139
In Praise of Lust 140
[the truth is] 141
[witch moon] 142
[the moon cups her hand to hold] 143
[small apple leaf that winces & grins] 143
[with her drunkest eyes   she would like to see] 144
Rose the Dyke 145
[do you come from this country?] 146
[her arm dangles along the shelf of my sleep] 147
[outside of flagstaff, arizona, at dawn:] 147
[moon stalking] 147
[what does she want?] 148
[i'll put it] 149
[on our love bed i imagine] 149
[but] 149
[near troutdale i should have] 149
[come to me when the moon is waxing] 150
[the mountain field opens ...] 152
[twenty miles from Mesa Verde] 153
[what's best] 153
[i light the candle of drunkness] 153
[thick against the screen] 154
[some   one] 154

[this is my vagina's song] 155
[sea underwind has] 156
Linda at Eight 156
[flight of ravens] 157
[diving,   i kiss and/kiss and/ kiss] 158
[i brush the windchimes with my shoulders] 158
Whale Poem 2: For She Who Still Thrives 159
[my love is amber] 160
[my love is copper] 161
[my love is rose] 161
[the flesh is a sweet river] 162
[if I put my hand on your belly   and my cheek] 164
[with its howls, its seas, its] 165

They Will Know Me By My Teeth Selections 165

In the Jewelry Room of the Egyptian Collection 169
What Can I Ask 171
New England Cemetery 174

Essay: *The Ex-Patriot and Her Name* by Elana Dykewomon 175

Afterword: *Wimmin, Words, and Wisdom: Elana Dykewomon and Communities of Lesbian Readers* by Julie R. Enszer 185

Elana Dykewomon Bibliography 193

Preface:
Elana's Garden in Belgrade

When I was very young, I used to listen secretly to late-night discussions by my parents about physics. I would go to sleep with strange words of *atoms and molecules*, *Marie Curie*, and *Newton's laws*. But never did I dream as a girl in the sixties in Belgrade, Yugoslavia, that one day I would encounter a poem where "A Law of Physics" would become a lesbian love story in the midst of the misogyny of the true tragedy of 1911, where the core of the famous law of mass and acceleration that my parents believed in would become an oath of lesbian love winning over death. "A Law of Physics," a masterpiece among Elana Dykewomon's poems, is about not only the law of physics, but the law of fathers and therefore the entirety of history. I read this poem not only as *disobedient to civilization*, but as an entrance to a new world of love of women that never before existed in this way, that never before we could even know how to dream it alone. *Nothing will be as sweet as the taste.*

Yes, I decided, in 2008, that we lesbians must translate this poem and show it to everyone we love.

The first time I saw Elana Dykewomon was in a book of photographs by Joan E. Biren. I bought *Making a Way: Lesbians Out Front,* (Glad Hag Books, 1987) at the famous *Sisterwrite* feminist bookstore in London during one of my hitchhiking journeys in Europe at the end of the eighties. I found both of JEB's books, this one and *Eye to Eye: Portraits of Lesbians* (1979), and ever after looked in awe and admiration, paging through each of them so many times until I remembered every face in there. The portraits of lesbians in these JEB books were the family I wished to have. I was on a way to become a feminist lesbian in Eastern Europe, and the image and the

name of Elana Dykewomon was one of those in my butch pocket. JEB's photograph showed a big woman with her tongue out, which I saw then as a lesbian mocking the core of heteropatriarchy, including my father the physicist.

The second time I saw Elana Dykewomon was in a cafeteria in Jerusalem in 2005 at the Women in Black International Conference. She was sitting at a table, very ordinary, having breakfast. I looked at her and thought, *I cannot believe it, I know this big woman from somewhere so close to my heart.* I just could not remember where I knew her from, while at the same time I knew her so well. Watching her eat, I also thought, *This woman is so famous in the lesbian world, how is it possible that all these lesbians sitting near me are not screaming her name out, or lining up in a queue to talk to her.* As I could not remember where do I know her from, I thought maybe she would know. I almost jumped to sit near her, telling her who I am, but that would not make any sense to Elana Dykewomon! *Hm,* I thought, *something is unusual here, I had to think fast: I know her well, she does not know me at all—so how did I meet her then, for goddess's sake?* But, as the laws of deduction and induction were my youth time friends, I had to reason: if not alive, I met this mega lesbian in a photograph! Then it clicked: Yes, the book. The Golden Photo Books of My Lesbian Childhood! I had found one of the book's characters in person, finally! Here she was: my lesbian-soul-family member popped out in front of me in her full smile. I was excited. Just imagine how excited I was! I looked Elana Dykewomon straight in her charming face. *My long-time longing sister is here.* I was not able to take my eyes away from her. Elana Dykewomon's smile growing even wider and more sparkling. Finally, I shouted, "The Book! I know you from the JEB book!"

"Ah good," she said.

Very easy the words came out of her, like spring water. She was smiling; I was smiling. The rest is a herstory of lesbian comradeship.

if the road is long enough
I think of every other woman I known

In our herstory, there are many warm moments of encounter. Elana driving me in her fast car, just like in the song of Tracy Chapman. Me sleeping in her "poet barn," a kind of a lesbian ashram, using these words to show how precious the lesbian barns are with lesbian books, lesbian memory objects, a large soft lesbian double bed to dive in . . . There in her poet barn, I finally started to read her fiction and poems.

Back home in 2011, some of us feminist lesbians we said, "Yes, we desire to have Elana in Belgrade." In 2010, we hosted Joan Nestle, so we started preparing for yet another *Lesbian Spring*. This time with Elana Dykewomon.

May 30, 2012 - Elana Dykewomon: Lesbian poetry evening in Belgrade.
From left: Desa Drobac, Lepa Mladjenović, Elana Dykewomon,
Azra Causević, Nina Djurdjević Filipović, Tijana Popivoda.

In 2011, we had already translated *Sister Outsider, Compulsory Heterosexuality and Lesbian Existence, Stone Butch Blues* and some stories by Joan Nestle and Sandra Butler into the Serbo-Croatian language. There are lesbian poets in our region, but the lesbian community never before had a chance to encounter a lesbian like Elana who tells the public "My career is to be a cultural worker in the women's and lesbian movements, acknowledging my identities as a Jew, a fat and old woman, disabled, peace and lesbian activist."

Six feminist lesbians fascinated with the politics of her identities and her writings formed the 'Elana Organizing Committee': Tijana

Popivoda, Desa Drobac, Jodie Roy, Suncica Vucaj, Nina Dj F (trans-
lation) and me. As usual, we met in cafes for long hours to hear
everyone and divide the tasks. We needed to resolve the core of
what is characteristic of Elana Dykewomon to make her work un-
derstandable for lesbians in the Serbo-Croat-Bosnian language. We
discussed:

Elana's last name. Why such a name? An invented last name
that says "no" and "yes" at the same time. Some of us were deeply
affected by the story of the name, the smashing of the patriarchy
to the root. But how to translate it? Do we translate it? Do we
assume everyone speaks English? Why should we? The old story
of how to translate poets. And who translates who? Marina Tzve-
tayeva, the most famous poet we hold in this part of the world,
is mostly translated by a few men poets into Serbo-Croatian. That
was the Russian language of the 1930s, but now we have a dyke
English language of 1980s.
   I dream about the traveler
   ashamed of her passport
   and afraid to travel without it

Elana's big body and fat poetry. Never before, that I know, has
any lesbian in such a body entered the lesbian scene in the Serbo-
Croatian-Bosnian language. What a powerful existence. Elana's
poems open words for slicing body and slicing food, for loving
and hating eating . . . all around capitalism and—yes, pleasure.
Poems giving no answers but new spaces of fear and hope. How
to transmit the depth of the personal demands to all those of us
who are eating every day?
   I am a fat womon...
   Why do I think I need to tell you how much sugar... I eat in a day?

**Elana's antiwar politics strongly interwove with love among
women**. We the "Elana Organizing Committee" are activists with
Women in Black Against War and Militarism. It is crucial for us to

know that war is relevant to lesbian writers, as the war in our region took ten years of our lives and war is going on in many places in the world now, but women loving women are hardly ever connected with wars. Because in the war zones, men and guns are the Rule, and so the ethical construction of the "victim" becomes untouchable by what are still in the patriarchal world "unethical and dirty lesbians and homosexuals." For us, Elana Dykewomon is the example of a lesbian who does not live in war zone, but who did care deeply for those of us affected by war. Lesbian solidarity in the heart of her creation.

After a year of planning, Elana Dykewomon arrived big and smiling. We had two unforgettable nights in Belgrade: a historic reading of poetry never heard spoken in this language before. Every single phenomenon and act uttered by her changed our eyes and ears. We lesbians were full of sparkles, laughter, and love. A young lesbian told me that night, "Everything she says is true, even if I never thought of it before."

The third day it was sunny in Belgrade, and we lesbians hung around for an entire day, moving from one cafe to another, sticking close to Elana Dykewomon, catching every one of her smiles to store them for later hard times.

if you were my home I would be your garden

Lepa Mladjenović
April 2015

Lepa Mladjenović is a feminist lesbian activist who has spent many years working as a feminist counselor for women who have suffered the trauma of male violence. Lepa cofounded many groups, among them for lesbians (Arkadia and Labris) and for violence against women (Autonomous Women's Center Against Sexual Violence). Since 1991 she has been an activist of Women in Black Against War, a feminist antifascist group in Belgrade, Serbia. Lately she is engaged with the issue of lesbians in the peace movement.

Introduction:
Rekindle the Spark, Ignite a New Fire

The 1970s and 1980s nurtured an amazing bounty of lesbian-feminist authors, none more accomplished and inspiring than Elana Dykewomon. She brought a strong sense of history to the mix, as well as an articulated Jewish perspective which helped broaden the base of liberation discussions. Those decades were a period when we regularly gathered at three-hour poetry readings that were as rousing as any political rally then or as any poetry slam is today. Women's words were fierce, provocative, and demanding. The mere act of coming together in a room and saying them out loud was revolutionary and even, for some, dangerous.

Television shows like *Charlie's Angels* and *The Dukes of Hazard* were still selling that old-time religion—patriarchy. At the same time, the Women's Press Movement was sparking the publishers and magazines which were snatching the covers off the beast of sexism so women would know it when we saw it.

Helen Reddy's anthem, "I Am Woman Hear Me Roar," elicited a lot of snickers from the radio disc jockeys (almost all male), but they had to play it because radio was still responsive to listeners and women were demanding it. Elana Dykewomon's roar has always been more the sound of a persistent and urgent stream carrying us toward the memories of our oppression that were often subsumed under the larger (read male) stories. Once immersed in the stream, we were able to find the current that helped us make it to the other side.

Her first two novels were groundbreaking and have sometimes defined her work for many readers. The first, *Riverfinger Woman* (1974), opened us up to an irresistible way of being—putting women at the center of our existence. It made us long for a place where women were challenged to look each other in the eye. The second,

Beyond the Pale (1997), is a tightly woven story of Russian-Jewish émigré women in the early part of the twentieth century. Its harsh realities and its tenderness are carefully drawn with the same close perceptions that make her poems so remarkable.

While fiction by lesbians was blossoming with hothouse speed in this period, poetry was the most prominent currency in the radical movement. Its rhetoric was succinct and rousing as it peeled back the layers of insult, violence, and diminution which molded women's roles into caricatures for generations. Feminist writers excavated the deep hole into which women's bodies had been tossed, and then carefully resurrected our history and our psyches so we could have a chance to be whole again.

Before the Internet, there was a web of women communicating with each other across the country and the world through writing. Each new poem from a favored author informed your own. Writers who emerged from movements—Feminist, Black, Native American, Jewish, Progressive—like Adrienne Rich (1929–2012), Audre Lorde (1934–1992), Judy Grahn (b. 1940), Irena Klepfisz (b. 1941), Marilyn Hacker (b. 1942), Pat Parker (1944–1989), Chrystos (b. 1946), Cheryl Clarke (b. 1947), Cherrie Moraga (b. 1952), and Kitty Tsui (b. 1952) held legions of women rapt with poems of lesbian love, desire, and liberation.

Elana Dykewomon (b. 1949) is a part of that weave. Her work stands as evidence of dynamic political and poetic activism as well as her deep personal commitment to literary craft. Elana's work takes many forms, but the shape of her poems is less important than the emotional and social impact of the words. "A Law of Physics," about the Triangle Shirtwaist Factory fire in 1911, holds the essence of the alchemy that is her poetry. The poem describes what it might have meant for two women workers to hold hands as they leapt to certain death, escaping from a locked factory floor when the building erupts in flames. Using the mathematical calculations for falling objects, Elana spins glistening gold that takes your breath away with its precision and its rawness when she makes us understand that "...no one knows the price of comfort..." In this early piece, ideas, images, and information are transformed into emotion. I've used the poem in every poetry workshop I've taught since I first heard it because of Dykewomon's ability to lock the reader into the horror of the circumstance and the tenderness within the falling.

In "big belly on the road from reno," she traces the travels of a woman making her way through a new landscape as many women were doing in their personal terrain. The speaker's emotional responses to her journey are as much formed by the history she can sense around her; the acceptance of the circumstances and women wherever she encounters them as they are by her own healthy size. Near the end, she states it easily: "...among the greatest gifts/is to be able to read a map/to place yourself on it..." And in "the real fat womon poems," Dykewomon tackles the paradoxical prejudice this hyper-consumer nation has against fat people—presumed to be super-consumers because of their size: "The fat womon, she'd do./She moves slow, and she's wide./It's her who starves children across the globe..."

At the same time, Dykewomon celebrates the joy of eating without guilt: "I am a lucky womon. If I lie in bed and have a fantasy/about eating six chocolate cakes/of being fed six chocolate cakes by six fat womyn/who are admiring my six new rolls of flesh/I can get pleasure from my fantasy..." In this mouthwatering rumination, she crushes the influence of Madison Avenue and media that dictate "0" as the size to which women should aspire. Zero has become another hole into which some women are thrown so that all other women are invisible.

Writing that is grounded in mythology is, of course, some of my favorite work. Her poem "Some notes on the nature of the bad queen" is composed of tightly written lines that examine the archetypal 'bad queens' of endless fairy tales. The poem exposes the mean spirit not of the queen but of those who construct her dubious character which has endured through time and becomes emblematic of how society often perceives any woman who is not a shrinking violet: "...she is always too beautiful too exotic/too vain too arrogant too greedy too pushy. Too much..." But who is this powerful women that so many are so afraid of her they must make her into a monster? Dykewomon ponders why in the stories: "No one brings her daisies..." And I think even Frankenstein's monster in the Mary Shelley novel was awarded a flower by the innocent girl child who is strategically oblivious to his bizarre features and brutal behavior. Dykewomon's poem reminds us that we cannot take these myths that demonize women's power at face value. If we question, then we can learn new truths about ourselves.

Sensuality is everywhere in her poems, even in the way she sees and touches bowls or wood or water. In expressly sexual poems such as the short piece "even my eyes become mouths" that sense of touch is especially vibrant. The title, with its provocative image, could—given a few more syllables—be an apt haiku unto itself.

Her new poems are direct descendants of her earlier work, maintaining her incisive style, animating curiosities, and sensual language while, in some cases, posing intellectual questions. In "When to answer," she explores how to respond to a man's letter from a literary magazine requesting she submit a poem for publication. Feelings of surprise and suspicion lead to a narrative about annoyance at being distracted from attending to women as well as the dangers of ignoring a request from a male. The poem's loose narrative threads through the story of this request to a final—almost breezy response—that masks the troubling reflections from which it emerges. This blend of ideas and emotion makes Dykewomon's poetry fulfilling and enduring.

An exciting addition to this collection is the final essay "The Expatriot and Her Name" which begins with a painfully simple and true sentence: "Names define reality." The essay, which originally appeared in *Inversions—Writings by Dykes, Queers & Lesbians,* describes the road Elana Dykewomon has traveled to being herself. With the essay, the reader develops a more direct and personal relationship to her and her poems that will, perhaps, send you back to read the poems again.

We've lost many of the voices who were part of that web of activism in the 1970s and 1980s. But their words are still with us in their books which line our shelves or sit stacked beside our beds. The heat from their words is still warm. This collection, *What Can I Ask*, will rekindle the spark for the lapsed poetry reader/revolutionaries of our generation and with any luck ignite a new fire in the next.

Jewelle Gomez
April 2015

Jewelle Gomez is a writer and activist and the author of the double Lambda Award-winning novel, *The Gilda Stories*, from Firebrand Books. Her adaptation of the book for the stage, "Bones & Ash: A Gilda Story," was performed by the Urban Bush Women company in 13 US cities. The script was published as a Triangle Classic by the Paperback Book Club. Gomez is the recipient of a literature fellowship from the National Endowment for the Arts, two California Arts Council fellowships, and an Individual Artist Commission from the San Francisco Arts Commission. She has served on literature panels for the National Endowment for the Arts, the Illinois Arts Council, and the California Arts Council.

New Poems

I have just begun this

Red stream of evening sky
                              the edge of my lands
     softened   on the horizon tomorrow's fog
     the rim she said   the world had been a bowl
     wooden or glass
                        all that confined us is
                                 shattered now
the coastal trees speak
                             at every moment of the tide
                             speak to me
                             we are together still
  without boundary
                   using faces landscapes
                   none of us recognize
                            but know
         our lands rising on the swell
         the ocean desert home
     high animaled wilderness   cities of red clay
        do not forget the journey
        not an inch of it   nor hour
              our calves bulge from the hike
              our minds
                      keen in grief
              for the canyon
              for the hometowns
              for the chants of womyn
              who bled freely
              into the soil   our soil
       do not stop now
                         speak to me
                         I need you
      I have just begun this song

Women in Black

The old women gather
they say
all things intersect
we stand at these crossroads
plaque in the veins of history
hey the young men yell
get out of the way you
wanna give us heart failure
your hearts have already failed
the old women respond
we are here to hold
the mirror
you had a choice
you chose death
but we are forgiving
choose again

Assignment

June 1997, as reported in the San Francisco Examiner*: A 25-year-old Kosovo Liberation Army officer, Fitnete Ramocaj, stated, "I am responsible for recording all the massacres in this region and this [at Lubenic] is the most terrible I've seen."**

I am twenty-five years old.
Before the war I liked to write poetry,
when the cherry trees sniffed
into season, or the plaited wheat —
Now poems are written by skeletons in mud.
Many other countries were interested in our war.
They voted in parliaments.
On our ground, both sides retaliate.
But the enemy retreats.
Now the captain says, "You, Ramocaj,
you like to write? We need you
to record the massacres.
Here's a camera, film, a fresh pad of paper —
good supplies. Be precise."

If I see a swarm of flies near the ground
I know I'll find bodies.
Bones lean out of mounds of charred hay
as if to wave or point out Serbs.
The ripe yellow plums in orchards
are bitter as refugees.
I make columns — men, women, children.
Most are indistinguishable.
Twenty-three bedrolls, fifteen knapsacks
in the plaza today.
When I unbuckle a strap, a toy bear falls out
made in China. Silverware. Computer disks.

* My friend Lepa Mladjenović in Belgrade did some research on this and found that Fitnete is a woman's name.

A survivor reports Serbs took corpses
away with tractors.

People will farm again here —
Albanians, Serbs, maybe a people
I can't imagine — and a plow
will slip its singing edge into a mass grave.
Europe must be larded with these pits,
mutual disintegration overcoming
forbidden intimacy.
I wipe my forehead. Cold winter, warm spring.
I count, turn the page, rule a new column.
My responsibility
is to record the massacres, they said.

Until they end?

Pauline Newman at 92♀
an opening monologue

The New York Fire Department
picks me up every March to wave
in the parade they have for that awful fire
— I sewed at Triangle, but after 1909
would never go back.

1911, I was organizing in Ohio,
so I survived.
Maybe it's being stubborn
that makes a long life.

They trot me out on Mayday and whenever
some union official hears I'm still
alive I have to give a speech.
I only have one speech anymore:

I was of the 1909 vintage
and I did my share, that's all.
Today workers watch Hollywood Squares
— we studied Tolstoy and Shelly by oil lamp.
Well, you're free to do
what you want with your hours
that's what we fought for but
won't you keep faith
keep faith with us who made the union strong?

♀ Pauline Newman was born c. 1890 in Kovno, Lithuania. She lived on 12th St. in Greenwich Village from the early 20's until 1983. She died in 1986 in the home of the daughter she had adopted with Frieda Miller, her life-long partner and New Deal economist. Rose Schneiderman was a labor activist and president of the Women's Trade Union League.
In the poem, "the union" is the International Ladies' Garment Worker's Union. "Triangle" refers to the Triangle Shirtwaist Factory Fire of 1911 - see page 59. "1909" refers to the mass strike of women shirtwaist workers in NY, the "Uprising of the 20,000." Direct quotes are taken from Newman's interviews and letters.

It's an easy speech because I iron
the complications out and make it smooth.

In the beginning I used to live in hotel rooms.
I'd write to Rose every day from the road —
"While my life, and way of living
is *very interesting* — *it is* at the same time
a very long life, always alone.
Except when you're out doing your work …
so much work to do — work
that shall *live* after I am gone
— yet no one to help me, no one to admire me."
I couldn't have been more than 22.

 "The shirtwaist factory was my college,
the union was my graduate school."

A person makes a little pantry of phrases,
rows of neat jars with the same
pickles and fruits. I take them out for company
with the delicacy interviewers expect
of an old lady. Lady!
I was never.

But it *is* long, life — as long now at ninety
as it was then. I've outlived
help and admiration.
Rose Schneiderman, my comrade and friend,
used to have tea with Eleanor Roosevelt at Hyde Park
— she was on Franklin's Labor Board but
we never rose as high as the "native born"
or our allies in the middle-class.

Allies — that's what I mean, make it smooth.
We used to infight, just like you.
Frieda was an economist
and the democrats loved her.

Together from 1917 until '69.
We raised a child. Our grandchildren
look at photos of Pauline Newman
for Sheriff of New York and
Frieda Miller with Truman.

She left me once — well, twice — we called it work.
But at the end, when she asked for me
I took pride in showing up.
Every day I went to the old age home.

Our time was different.
I don't give you permission
to sensationalize this, smother us
in your new vocabulary. Or even to quote.

I lived the best way I could. At 17, I ran
for New York Secretary of State
on the Socialist ticket.
70 years with the union,
but I had to live past 80 to see
the first woman on the executive board.

Out on the road I had a photo
of the union brass I'd hold up for the girls —
what's wrong with this, I'd ask.
Finally I had to say — you can see it!
They're all men.

They put me in the Education Office
of the Health Department — at first
I thought it was exciting but long before
my fifty years were up I knew
how badly my energy, my knowledge
were being used.

A lousy trick. Sometimes Frieda would
get me on a council, commission — those people

should have been out on the streets, not
nodding at testimony. They'd treat me
like a tough old aunt —
tell us a story about the unions, auntie.

There are times I'd like to shut the door,
throw these old preserves against the wall.

Rose did, you know — after McCarthy
she got afraid, destroyed almost everything —
mementos, love letters, socialist arguments.
There weren't more than twenty at her funeral —
no different at the end —
not for Rose, probably not for me.

So I have a simple speech I want to make,
that's all. If I could
I would stand up in my grave
and if I couldn't stand, I would sit on the stone
and tell all the people who came by

what it was like in 1909
when the women went on strike —
the knife you can be, organized.
The working woman needs a wage
that guarantees more than survival.
Keep faith with me.
Women need a decent quality of life.

Butch resisting the pressure to change gender♀

Everyone has a little story to tell
and words are usually in it

my word is a chanterelle
a pulpy flair on the forest floor
                                    yes it is   yes it is
my word is golden seal   it's
serious   all medicine   count on me
                                    oh do   do please
we are the words we know
juxtapose   obfuscate
collision   labia
     so many words are delicate & strong
     moss agate   rutile
     aurora borealis
                                    delicate   shadowy
     zion canyon lit by headlight   why does everyone
          want to tell the story   in gender   at the end?

breasts/no breasts
     packing   passing   lipstick
                    the words   are rude
                    long past when rudeness
                    should be wonder
what kind of awe
          opens membrane up   sifts   small particles
makes us   useful –
     snap dragon delilah pudding jazz horned owl what

♀ I have been thinking about gender—thinking, reading, listening deeply—all my adult life. This is one attempt to puzzle it out, since I cannot find in myself a sensation of "feeling like a woman" or "feeling like a man" that is other than having a female reproductive system, and having to choose one or the other has always seemed too limiting. Yet I am part of a culture that systemically, hierarchically, violently oppresses females and have spent my life loving women.

opal   fossil   fret   dulcimer   makes up sex
                  why is everyone
                  so stuck
                  on the mirror

(because she knew an old friend /
because she heard many lesbians butch women
wanted their breasts cut off & did:
because it seems betrayal   not
just the obvious   butch, comrade
     trying to survive as womon   dyke
     living as if a dyke could live   but
this other part:
           wasn't it   for liberation
                 didn't we march & marching
                 mean more than slogans
                 mean more than hormones
                 freedom to choose
                 a medicalized life

wasn't it   to be able to press our palms
         against a woman's flesh   & speak
              blueberry speak
              tunnel   speak
              spruce space for the body we get born to

   it's the tender story   we make
                   (remember we
we were many & went out   with baskets
to take in the lost sparks from fireworks
& use them to burn a boundary   & we tried to say
home   say   safe))
              is it me
       who doesn't understand anymore
       the narrative thread gone

        men can be what they want to
        but mostly they have been the same

why bother
    to look as if
    you could join them
   where's the jingle the jiggle the clover of that
       is looking good in a suit
      an answer to what question

    & somewhere in there
    disappointment takes out its knife
       pretty knife steel toledo
          switch blade
      graft knack
hacks the body up
        it was just
        a woman
        what good
        is a story like that?

When to answer ♀

Your postcard last November read:
Please send me some/one of
your own poems for
publication in our Spring
issue —
                    I am always surprised
when men are aware
of the work I do
and if flattered
also suspicious   should I
turn away from womyn
even for the length of this poem?
I know womyn are opening
your magazine but
it's you who are asking.

I keep the postcard and forget it
until my father gets a cancerous tumor
that shuts the breath out of him and I
have to deal with my brothers.
                    My brothers remind me
how dangerous it is
refusing men.

            One of them wrote me three letters:
First: I haven't seen you in eight years
I want a sister, I want to know what a sister means.
After three months or so: Okay at least you
could answer me   don't I deserve an answer
who do you think you are?
And then: I had a dream about my penis and it was
at the racetrack and now it's in your house

♀ From a request from *ZYZZYVA*, and published there in 1994.

here it is my penis is in this letter
so fuck you if you don't want to write me back.

Once as an experiment in an ice cream shop
with two other lesbians we didn't
respond to a man who asked us what time it was.
Within five minutes he was talking to himself and
calling us dyke bitches   damn bra burners —

I used to think this was interesting but now
I've known too many attacked womyn
read too many newspapers.

I am not asking for it
not asking for anything
here's your poem.
I have to get back to work now
alright?

Unravel, then

My father taught the names
of constellations: Orion, Cassiopeia,
Seven Sisters. He was a flight navigator
in the war.

At a classmate's farm in Oregon
we ate venison her husband shot
took her three year old down the steps
into the dark yard –

"What are those? What are those!"
terrified, pointing up to the night from
the hammock of her mother's arms.
Why

do we still draw lines
making maps with figures from
Greek mythology? We are far
from Greece.

Coastal dark not quite
as light polluted as any city. Look up –
Pete Seeger holds his guitar, Marion
Anderson sings

on the steps of the Lincoln
Memorial – see? Barbara Jordan lectures
congress and the Seven Lesbian Poets take
their place:

June Jordan, Adrienne Rich, Audre Lorde,
Gloria Anzaldúa, Muriel Rukeyser,
Paula Gunn Allen, okay, Sappho.
Then

my father lays a 20-year dead hand
on me, says: I taught you these. These
are the names. Renaming the world
is a conceit

you've suffered for a long time. Stop
suffering. Accept this sky. We've
tamed the night, haven't we? You should know
from your mythology

when you pick at a thread
the whole thing
starts unraveling.

California

After the earthquake
a man on an estuary
called the news —
he happened
to glance out his window
at the moment
every bird
sprinted skyward
one solid lift of wing
and this
was before
he felt — or heard —
the lurch.

The world will end
like this: us stuck
while what is wild
moves up
without considering
perch.

dream fish

Here's a fish tank filling half a room
some sudden wave of derision
some current of fission
blows them out of the water

I gather up all I can
return them but hours later
remember — parrotfish?
the tank seems sparse

under the bed I discover
tiny sea ferns, nudibranchs, slugs &
anemones & the parrotfish, baby flounder
all caught in a net of belief that,

because they can still
see each other,
they can somehow breathe
the alien air

even those gasping
on the periphery
recover, startled, as I place them
back in water

the tank gets murky,
chaotic with activity —
I miss the momentary clarity
of fish swimming in oxygen

maintaining careful position:
as long as they could see each other
they might survive and
drowning remain a fiction

Now about old women —

If genetic memory exists
and our mothers' blood
stamps us with specific
fear of strangers, of eclipse,

pogroms – or maps
survival – knowing how
to swim upstream & when –
consider this:

motherhood stops at 30
40, tops – we don't get a code
for being old
we have to make it up

no pattern for age shies
in a recessive gene
the old can't be recognized
so it's just   shut us up or out

but hey and hi diddly
we drink martinis
speak in tongues   profanities
plot more than gardens

– old women tell the truth
beyond allegiance to dna
or manipulation by
tv conspiracies

no one is born
knowing the taste
of old knowledge but we're
dangerous   delicious

invite us in

Nothing Will Be As Sweet As the Taste

selections

If you were my home
I would be your garden

If I was your garden   I would want you
to cultivate me to plant water weed harvest
and like I promised   I would feed you

You can always eat what straggles up or
what's gone to seed but   nothing will be
as sweet   as the taste of the womon
you tended purposefully

she says she is

she says she is air   she says she is fire   she says she is water she
says she is earth
        then they laugh at her   they say:
                                you are not all these things
let's see your chart
produce your papers   sweetheart
and your past

        but my past did not imagine me here
                on the edge of cliffs
                                        at the boundary of air
                        making fire out of water
                knocking on the hearts of metal and wood

        and flesh of course flesh

                                    which is the lesbian   element

they forget to mention

A lesbian's prerogative

It's a lesbian's prerogative to run her hand down the seam
    across the seam of need
    and stick her finger in
    where the stitch is loose

a lesbian prerogative
    to pull at the thread, rip it apart
    demand the womyn
    start over

a lesbian prerogative to name herself:
        I am here before
        naming begins before
        phyla and genera   I am
    the species who laughs
        looking at herself in the water
        who crows across the
        the river basin: beware
            my name is hot pepper and sea salt
        my name is spice
        I must be used
        with knowledge of effect
    I change the chemistry
        of the day I enter
        I am the hidden reactor
        I have a half-life of millennia

I can be forced   turned to stone
    underground   I can be hidden
    in storehouses   untapped
    my name can be erased from
    the pillars and tombs
                still I come back

I am the lesbian lesbians are afraid of —
                    the one who says
                    you can't have it easy

                    it doesn't work both ways there's
                    no polite company   no
                    diligence with which
                    you can coin a phrase
                    that will change the root
                        of men's culture
                                    and make it safe

it's a lesbian prerogative
        to prophecy
        to rant and demand
        a clear enemy defined
        when she becomes a moving target
        to expect her friends
        to track the source
        of what harms us

it's a lesbian's prerogative
        never to apologize
        to rip at the seams until
        she's satisfied
        and, once satisfied,
                        to doubt satisfaction
                        and start again.

Knowledge in the Biblical Sense

To know her as if in pages. Not any pages. The great pages. To
know her among the great pages, where everything is important,
everything matters. Will matter, for centuries.
So that, if I say, behold
thy skin shines as foam on the scales of an asp
hundreds of scholars
will debate my meaning, the gesture, the state of mind,
the ancient fortress so long abandoned —
and the garden, what herbs grew there?

To know her in the biblical sense,
verse and line of her creases under the
sensitive skin of my thumb, the page
beginning to soften with age, the paper
sending a humming vibration, so that, looking up
toward the light in the library window, I am
overcome with sensation that starts
one hundredth of a cubit above my knees,
and an angel speaks out of the light
lo, you are full of passion,
your dwelling is touched by desire, you must
make a covenant, a promise, a sacrifice

in order to so change the meaning of scripture

you
must know   what route lust goes as it travels to love
and how it touches the imagination of your people
to beget
your people
one by one

by knowing her in pages
and making known what is known

throwing the book open
    to our own interpretation
                yes, I am pleased
                I knew her that way

on land, in the mythical city
    where her hands shaped monuments of clay
    around which naked girls sang
    after the battle, in the midst of harvests
                    ripe and full
        handing me the page

      I am satisfied
      I knew her
          that way

Carnal Knowledge

First we had the sacred, and then the profane. Biblical,
then carnal. Sacred, then profane. What's the
difference? she mumbled into my neck,
right after her tongue slid out of my ear.
                                    I'll tell you, honey
                        I wanted to say, but
my mouth was full of her lips, and I was shaking with
five pleasures at once.
                I could see it though. I mean everyone
knows about me by now, how I stroke my chin in the
middle of Trivial Pursuit, discussing the answer, and
they laugh, saying, well, nu, rebbi?

        So, nu, the sacred is easier to describe than
the profane: The sacred comes across the plains
of time smelling of sandalwood, beating a tambourine,
and her dark hair falls as water over sense — opening the
passages to revelation, bridging the sensate world with
the world of prayer, so that every touch is an act of
devotion, of affirmation, of celebration in the spirit of the
universe, the power that moves mountains and shakes
seas is gratified by our union,   and after our union,
our reflection upon it — the way what is sacred takes
hold of us and gives depth and connection to the holy,
the creative unfolding of our days.

        Say that again she said   Mmmmmmph, I said
No, she said, pushing her hand deep into my thigh,   Say
what you want.
                        I want you   I said
Where she said   In me   I want you in me
I want you hard in me   I said
                How hard? she said   Harder
I said   I was sweating and shocked, grabbing at the flesh
of her upper arms, wanting more and more of her and I

could see her: how she'd just been, how I had been
between her legs and my whole hand was throbbing in
her cunt/ I had been eating her but now
I had one hand moving and twisting, calling to her to
open to me   and one palm pressing against her clit,
against the mound, deep into the bone, the way
the brown skin of her thigh creased and winked
made my hips writhe and I ached to fuck her better than
I ever had   deeper strong entirely
present in my lust, wanting to make her forget
everything but wanting and she was calling my name,
saying fuck me, fuck me   yes   and I was saying   it's
so good   you're so good I love to fuck you and then she
was in me saying:
                            What's that you said?
                                    Tell me what you want

                                        I was scared to death but
I said it, I was lying there saying fuck me, get inside me,
do me good —

                                        and
that's carnal knowledge. Just the tip of it too.
Even though we say the same words over and over it's
a lot more complicated being profane than being
sacred.
                            I mean
                        getting known
                    isn't something I learned
                        in Sunday School

The Census Taker Interviews the 20th Century

I came to her door in late afternoon.
It was August, she had planted roses
along a path of paving stones, out of date
and affected. The bushes still in bloom
were going past, the smell as ghastly as
roof pitch in that heat.
There was a brass knocker
in the shape of a mermaid. Cloying, I remember
I thought, annoyed by mounting evidence
of sentimental materialism. These little things
you can't write in your report
give so much away.
She took her time. Some
of my predecessors had praised her
as energetic, bustling; one
found her lists of patents brilliant. A famous
conversationalist in her youth, the last surveyors
found her quarrelsome and trite. Likely

I would be the last. I don't mind. Demographics
are the heart of our times, and I love a shift
in the underpinnings of alliance. I was prepared
for the crone, offering platitudes and
self-serving reminiscences. She demanded
my ID before unbolting an assortment of locks.

"Surprised,
aren't you?" A woman in her early twenties
sat before me in a platinum wheelchair. "Come."
She wheeled forty yards down a dark wood-paneled hall,
stained with the stink of onions and garlic. "Can't get
that smell out, believe you me, I've tried everything."

I expected photos, plaques, a velvet portrait
of Castro, Freud or JFK, a bad copy of O'Keefe,
but there was only odor. As we moved,
the odor grew, shifted, changed. Buttery
as a June night by a back-country Idaho lake it
would suddenly burn, ache or gag.
"Like I said, tried everything."

              We came to a room
with a glass wall overlooking a concrete patio,
around which cluttered an assortment of
neon and chrome statues. "It was a garden
during the war." When she laughed I could see
her face was thick with make-up. Not hiding
wrinkles, but covering large welts and sores.

"Which war?" she said, mocking me before
I asked. "Let's see, the war to end all wars or
the one for a new world order, or maybe it was
a victory garden, or perhaps I had it paved
after the Boxer rebellion — did we have concrete
then? Of course. You choose, whatever's
convenient."

            I was looking for the page
of my forms on diagnosis, trying
to decide between "senile dementia" "post-
traumatic stress" and "hysterical conversion"
when she said, "Don't bother. I may be sick
but my mind's still strong, and what's

wrong with me isn't listed in your papers."
There's a little box for "complex of
undetermined emotional/physiologic origin"
where I put a check. I had to get on with
the questions. "How many people

live in this house?"
                    "You children
always ask the obvious. Go ahead, look around,
count," her gesture arched
across flowered wallpaper, old
brown furniture with brass rivets.
There were square spots where
paintings had been removed.
"Look again," she said.

Now I saw ghosts in the chairs,
playing cards on the camelback couch.
Mediterranean women in shirtwaists and
others with rags around their dreads, tall
white men fiddling with watch chains and
men who had clearly died at the bottom
of mines in Ireland, Capetown, Tennessee.

In a flickering circle, as if through a stereopticon,
the shades of women were marching
for the union, the vote, revolution,
peace, civil rights, for control
of their bodies and sexuality.
"If it's a man's world, at least
I organize the parades — but there,
                    look
there —" she gestured at the walls.
What I had taken for flowers were head upon head
of generations. All the races of women
whose eyes demanded to transmit a
particular reality, children both starving and
well-fed, every kind of administrator, clerk,
laborer vied for my diminishing clarity.

"Well, of course I've had a family, but now
I'm happy to live alone." The images broke apart
with her voice, and I noticed with relief

the gleam of her simple, polished piano.
"Occupation?"

"Let's say I — sing, yes,
quite well. Do you know the Marseillaise? My
grandmother taught it to me, it's one of my
favorites but I can do Billie Holiday or
rock opera as easily. Would you
care for me to sing to you?"

This time I was
quick. "No. No, what's your source of income?"
"Income! Darling I manufacture tiny chips!"
She laughed again. "All over the globe
I have my fingers in. In China, North and South
Africa, Germany, Mexico — anywhere I can I
set up my new clean factories. We make
lasers the size of atom wafers. There is
a constant increase in my annuities. I may be
dying, but I've invested well.

You seem so
uncomfortable — it's hot in here, isn't it? I
don't like the air conditioner, I never felt
it was one of my better inventions — oh, it
works all right I suppose but that terrible
sensation of living with all the windows closed
as if nature were laying siege — of course it
did, for a decade or two, but we've gotten
beyond that, haven't we, we've made — progress."

She held my eyes. Sweat carved
the flesh on my back and under my breasts. The
smell returned in patterns, now pine-scented,
now something rotten, or a low sour wave of ash.
"You're not trapped, you know, you
are free to leave. You're able, mobile —"

I remembered my forms. "Oh. Disability. Your
disability is work, accident or genetically

related?" This time the laugh stayed
in her cheeks. "All," she said.
"I lost the use of my legs in Phnom Penh,
or was it in that fishing boat
off the coast of Hiroshima? A factory
explosion near Leningrad you never
read about? The Chicago doctor gave my mother
tranquilizers when she carried me. Really —
it's an act of god, don't you think?"

"Right — religion?" She stopped smiling completely.
"I used to. Very self-righteously. My children, some of them —
I tried a few ancient rituals in the last
years but I — the closer I am towards the end,
the less I believe."
                              "Still, you must have been
born into some faith?" "I was, exactly,
born into some faith. But I consider this question
an invasion of my privacy." We have our instructions.
I had to let it go but by then I thought
I was on to something.
                              "And don't you
want to know why I haven't aged?"
"Yes, but you just called me prying."
"It's my prerogative, isn't it? Anyway
it's only a trick done with mirrors. Look."
An invisible control turned the dimmer
switch. Even in the bright light she
didn't look more than thirty. Thirty and sick.

"And you want to know about *my* faith!
In 1903 when babies were thrown onto
bayonets, people in their outrage said
'To think this can happen in the 20th century!'
Everyone wants to think their age
the most modern. You are not exempt.
Here I am, your 20th century girl. Tell them

I had a wonderful singing voice, that
I was forever young."

On the small table
by her side there was a single stone, and she
started to roll it in her palm. "I think it's
time for you to leave." We went back
through the corridor, but now each inch
was hung with photos of politicians and
framed newspaper advertisements
for every car ever manufactured in the world.
There was a reek of sulfur, and then
fresh bread.
"Thank you," I said, when the
bolts were all unfastened and I could fix
on the familiar, unwavering stench of
overripe rose. "My pleasure. I'm always
glad for guests. I want to give you
a little going away present."
She put
the stone she had been fiddling with
in my hand. "A friend of mine, a child
survivor of the Warsaw Ghetto uprising,
went back to see Treblinka, she and
her mom, the last of her family. She sent me
this. I think you should have it. A
legacy, and all you had to do
was your job. Don't worry, no risk."

She wheeled the chair around
and locked the door. I put the papers in
my briefcase and stared at a cloudless sky.
The stone burns in my fist.

A Law of Physics♀

Saturday, March 25,1911

One body falling alone is its own weight
times distance.
Two bodies falling alone are their own but
if they hold hands
their weight is multiplied.

Here's a for instance:
Two girls are on a ledge.
The building is burning.
There are nets below.
The girls are young and for the purpose
of this example
thin and frightened.
It is eight stories to the ground.
The net can hold 90, 120, 150 pounds
times the distance but
holding hands
they become 11,000 pounds on impact.
The net breaks.
No one knows the price
of comfort,
how much they loved each other
and expected, by jumping,
neither to live nor die
but fly
released
from the Triangle Shirtwaist Factory.

♀146 workers, almost entirely Jewish and Italian women, died within 18 minutes during the Triangle Shirtwaist Factory Fire. The high death rate was attributed to not following safety and fire regulations, including the company's policy of keeping the fire doors locked to prevent employees from "sneaking out." Over 120,000 people marched in the funeral procession. This tragedy reoccurred in 1993 in a toy factory outside of Bangkok—fire, locked doors, jumping women, over 200 dead. And will keep reoccurring until we...

fifteen minutes from the kar kare klinic♀

JEWS should not live where I live
on the coast of oregon   we should move somewhere
when I was a kid
they said l.a. was safe, but it isn't anymore
not safe for kids' windows to sport menorahs
in new york where my grandmother
was an old jewish woman
a gang of white girls pushed her
into the gutter, broke her hips

they paint it on the sides of buildings
all over the states
all over the world
it keeps on reappearing
doesn't go away
every other day I clip it out of the newspapers
once we were in the flamingo cafe in new orleans
a group of highly painted secretaries were talking
—mama knows all about the jews   she dated one—

it's
easy to make this list
places where jews should not live:
in germany   in egypt   in portland
in yreka   in utah   in paris
in ghettos
outside of big cities   like skokie
in cuba   in the south
even miami isn't so great

♀ Between 1979 and 1983, my partner, Dolphin, and I were the only Jewish lesbians on the southern Oregon coast for hundreds of miles. The Kar Kare Klinic was owned by the organization its initials indicate. Shortly after this poem was written, the lone Jewish tailor in town (fifteen minutes in the other direction) had his shop burned down. In 1983, we moved to Oakland. This poem is not intended in any way as a justification for "the Jewish right of return."

in oakland they bait jews at their workplaces
& I don't expect it's easier in uganda
new zealand any
catholic protestant muslim or hindu nation
in russia the ukraine
in spain algeria chile bolivia buenos aires
el salvador nicaragua cape verde
south africa canada poland
a jew should not live alone
a jew should not live with other jews
it provokes attention
a jew should not live in the native lands of others
a jew should not live in israel
jews aren't israelis, they're just immigrants
they should have stayed out
should have stayed out of boston
out of singapore and canton
they should get out of california

and we should leave southern oregon

desire, jews, casino

I

she dreams of dripping water
a flooded race track.
the bets are all
in a foreign language which
might be spanish might be hebrew she isn't sure
she hasn't studied
when her grandfather was alive
they came out to the track
like a picnic, like a baseball outing
jews like to gamble a friend says
where you find casinos
there are jews
the week in tahoe didn't go well still
she picked up the tip to
always play machines
near the doors or food lines
the house likes noisy visible scores

tonight she has an urge to get back in the car
and drive up there
the middle of the night who cares now
there's a day's food in the feeder for the cat
she could go anywhere
tired of desire being attached to womyn
you can attach desire
to four of a kind to a royal flush
desire is like a leech it can fasten its mouth anywhere
it doesn't really need flesh or touch
the rough hull of a boat will do any fast car anything
shiny that moves

II

was that you?
complaining about desire?
complaining about desire and being a jew?
wanting a quick risk
a way to beat the odds
wagering what you get from the culture's hate:
 'o you jews are all so smart'
against your own fear of loss —
quick — watch those cards
it can be gone in a flash
or is it guilt, jew, to have even a week's worth of extra cash
here
take it,   enmesh me endlessly in this drama
about jews and money

about america and money about jews and america and money
the big casinos on the western lake
knowing just how much we can afford to lose
balancing loss against win
fear of money and the true sins of money
with the fear of death
of growing old in debt
fear of the knock on your door   genetic
fear of not having a bribe ready
when they come for you

III

or was it lesbians and desire?
would you start across the valley, into the sierra at midnight
because you don't live with your lover anymore
because you have no lover and you're tired of lovers
and you wish your old lovers
still wanted to touch you

wish you still wanted to touch them
wish that desire wasn't such a leech
siphoning vitality from your veins

until what's left is a collection of games
you can't bear to play
facing anyone more intimate than the dealer
the dealer doesn't know you
but she knows your face
she can see in your face desire's ash
rolling for a seven, laying a stack on twenty-two
gambling is something you can do with your hands

you know it.   tonight you resist the desire
to blow it shooting craps until four
but it doesn't change the way desire has you pacing
tracing your shadows in blood
you want
to take your desire
and attach it
once and for all to belief
on something that's safe
if not as bright as a slot machine,
if not as beautiful as her face,
then you demand
to desire yourself
want to believe you can own
your own reactions

you're still that naive

IV

o midnight eye
scowling across my dreams

I have a hard time losing money to machines
though I do it now and then
waiting for the perfect chance
and even if I say
there's nothing useful in romance
if it came gleaming through the night
if she smiled at me just right
I'd go

haven't I written this poem before?

it's so easy to repeat yourself in midlife
waiting for the trick the knack
the winning streak that
leads out of the casino

big belly on the road from reno

big belly rides around america
eating potato chips
enters the mountains
where she's slit branches
off sage plants
native american lesbians say
don't harvest the sacred sage
she wonders if this means
for personal use too
for the smell of it
hanging up, drying in her room
all these acres of
nothing but sage
and lizard and rock
she has sage from the last time
out on the porch but it's true
she doesn't light it as often
doesn't stop this time
so many things
that deal with smell and smoke
are traditions
this great west
is not her country
if the west is not her country
and new york is sepia memory
then she has none
she leaves the plants alone

***

waiting at home there's a message
on her answering machine:
send money to: an address:
for dykes who were run off land
in southern oregon

by organized aryans
because the dykes were jews
were jews and lesbians
run off: swastikas painted on their land
guns shot
on both sides   in the air.
big belly has been to reno and lost money
on a roll of dice
a hand of cards.

***

later big belly is on
the other side of the mountain
the potato chips are gone
when she stopped for dinner
by a nearly dry creek
there was a sound of cowbells above her
and the wind shaking alder leaves
she sat in her tank top
on a granite bolder
a fat lesbian eating the half sandwich
that came with the potato chips
thinking
what a lucky life
this is

***

in the valley there are orchards
irrigation makes this possible
she loves to travel
to make the twilight curve of earth
her habitation

big belly wishes for a minute
she had been a farm daughter
brave in the dimming smudge

under thick fruit awnings
staking out the shapes
of childhood phantoms
in that fantastic shade

***

the first time they drove by copperopolis
big belly said: copper-op-olis!
copperopolis! let's
check it out.
(you have to turn left off route four
go west into town
which is tucked into an elbow of earth
as the sierras taper down to
the great growing valley —
copperopolis the last mining village
on the map   the next name
is farmington.)
but her lover said:
no. I know enough about the life
of women in small towns.
I don't have to go out of my way
to look at another one.

the women? big belly hadn't given them
the thought. she was hoping for
rock shops and mining shafts,
ma's hometown diner, a great
hardware store stocking
jeans in every size. the women?
their lives?
this time she's alone and
makes the turn. in copperopolis
there's a bar with a sign:
minors expressly forbidden.
a general store that rents videos,
two guys playing checkers

in front of the fire station,
neat little houses wide spaced,
dotted, almost, along the road
she turns around in front of the old armory:
bingo 1st and 3rd saturdays.
driving back to route four
the woman   is there
on the deck in front of the bar,
a thin white woman in a loose print dress,
opening the door.

***

across the highway,
walking down a side street,
a young couple and their labrador.
it's not just Willa Cather updated,
it's video disks and home computers,
mail order business an hour
from stockton and   women
living in rural places
with men and dogs.

***

it gets dark in the valley.
she puts a tape on to keep awake
everything poignant and damp
with the changing light
the car goes up and down
waves of land   accurately
she appears to be steering
through liquid
some golden stubble of substance
that heaves upward and subsides
burnt patchy black along its crest
then flattens to fields

glass, she thinks, but doesn't know why.
glass reminds her of love
of knowing womyn
of how many womyn
whose transparencies
she felt she could read
if not like glass
then layers of rock on an exposed ridge
each layer set down by elements
thrust up by force,
dramatic events, the record clear
if you put your mind to it
and studied striation

but you were something else entirely,
she says to a ghost in the car,
more like mud
— oh mud, how flattering —
not that kind of mud,
the kind that's left
at the bottom of strong coffee
the essence from which
everything derives flavor
then you swirl what's left
to tell the future —
something big belly could never do
no matter how many times
she looked thoughtfully
deep into the cup

***

big belly remembers an invitation
to talk to elementary school children.
—what would I say to them?

—whatever you want.
then I would talk
poetry and geography
how among the greatest gifts
is to be able to read a map
to place yourself on it
and know which roads
are fastest
which the most absorbing

and then: the way your mother sings
or doesn't sing to you
all of that
will form layers and make you
your own place

excavate and explore
in order to find who's story
your life is telling

poem for my unborn niece

They'll say you have an aunt in california
I'll send presents
stuffed animals   an erector set
They'll say
your aunt is fat, she's a writer, she was supposed to be
the smart one in the family
but she never made much money.
I'll send you a picture   I'll be almost grey by then
and you'll swear you never saw
such a big womon   smiling
They'll say   she never married
When you're older
they'll tell you   or a cousin will whisper
at someone's bat mitzvah
Your aunt in california — she's a lesbian
It will seem mysterious, dangerous, eccentric,
an ancient shadow, a story
grownups know the end of and they won't tell
I'll write you a letter
I'll say it's true   I'm a fat lesbian,
and I'll tell you the stories of womyn
living mysteriously   in a dozen countries
if you tell me yours

come visit me

the real fat womon poems

I.

I went to get a glass of water
and was overtaken by grief
grief at the kitchen sink
womyn's grief
for the life that vanishes
hot water and grease
for the hundred fears
about what we eat
and what size we are
and whether standing,
with soap lining the creases of our hands,
hurts our backs or feet
and if that's our fault.
It was dark in your kitchen.
You had been complaining
about your body,
bitter attacks on the new swells
that define your belly and hips.
And I said
so why don't you hack yourself to pieces?
And you said   I wish I could.
When I got to the sink
I couldn't turn the faucet on.
The white porcelain dull
under the light from the yard
couldn't speak
my back to you
my back against the world
grief at the kitchen sink
a womon's drama
the fat womyn's fight

the silence we were born into
catching us.

II.

Will the real fat womon please stand up?
We want to take a good look at you.
Don't you trust us to look?
What is it you think will come to focus,
where do you think we'll begin?
With your double chin, the roundness of your cheeks,
the width of your upper arms—there
does the flesh ripple, or are they full?
Do they bulge, are they smooth?
Where are your stretch marks?
Did you gain weight fast or slow?
Do you eat a lot at once or
do you eat a little all day long?
We all know a fat womon is
what she eats.
Can we watch you eating?
You must be hiding something
in your flesh,
is it rage or sex?
C'mon, we're your friends,
we just care about you and we want to see
where the fabric hugs the expanse of your stomach
the rolls at your waist
the fat that collects in pockets on your upper back.
What kind of stomach do you have?
High and round, or does it slip, slowly,
toward your knees, do your nipples
scratch the top of your pants?
Do your pants fit?
When your clothes are too tight

do you feel like you're
exploding out of them
into the street
and all you want to do is
get out of sight?

III.

Asshole, asshole,
I can answer for myself,
you don't know anything
You ask these questions
as if I were an interesting specimen
as if I wasn't you
Who did this to us?
And what makes you think
I would ever trust you?

IV.

There is being fat,
and there is eating.
There is eating, and
then there's the food.
There is fat and
there is aging
There is aging
and there is disability.

None of these things
are the same things
though they are used,
often, interchangeably.
Who did that?

Who did that to us?
And with each of these words
is the word: ugly.
Even with the word
eating, the word ugly is paired
by womyn
in north america
in the late 20th century.

V.

Now there are politics
for these things.
Unpopular politics,
but there are some.

We live in a country
that consumes,
that needs consumption
to continue consuming,
and what gets consumed
are the resources and the lives
of dark skinned and poor people,
the lives of women in sweatshops,
of women carrying rocks on their heads
in india to build american hotels.
We saw a lot of newsreels in the '60s.
Some of us stopped watching the news
but the news doesn't change.
Even if I choose carefully,
don't want my "major purchases"
to contribute to the evil
done to people in soweto,
some woman in a factory
compromised her eyes or her lungs

her back or her labor
for my computer
for your vcr
for the stereo, hell, for the music.
When did we let ownership
purchase our analysis?
Consider it: they don't have to buy us out
we pay them.

It would be nice to have a target
an easy simple target   who could take
some of this unease
about our consumerism.
The fat womon, she'd do.
She moves slow, and she's wide.
It's her who starves children
across the globe
it is her hideous appetite
that makes us ashamed to be americans.
All those fat cats living off the fat of the land
we don't have access to,
the fat cats who are
lean men in limousines.
We call them fat
because we have been taught
that fat means eating
means consuming
means taking the rights to what is not yours
and these things which are not the same things
become the fat womon's fault
it's a shame she's so out of control.
We hope she stays indoors.

VI.

Oh, those politics
I thought you were going to talk

about the other stuff.
What other stuff?
You know, the stuff about the diet industry
and the stuff about women
hating ourselves
wanting to hack off parts of our bodies
sew our mouths shut
pull out our intestines
suck the fat with syringes
wrap ourselves in constricting plastics
take drugs that make our hearts race
race away from us.

VII.

In the zoo they have signs
polar bears may weigh up to half a ton.
A girl is reading the sign out loud.
"Wow!" she says.
We are standing there admiring the polar bear
who is doing back flips in her pool.

If they stuck a sign on the human race
and said members of this species
occasionally reach a weight of 1,000 pounds
but weights in the range of 1–400 are most common
would that help?

VIII.

Saturday afternoon, doing errands,
I catch pieces of a radio speech
on power relations.
A woman is talking about

the pleasures of mutuality,
not power over, but power with.
How we might better express power to our benefit
by touching and being touched
hugging and being hugged
feeding and being fed.
On the radio she said
it is a good and mutual pleasure
to feed and be fed.
I catch my breath.
Is it still possible
to transmute
the power relations
around eating
so there is
mutual pleasure left?

IX.

I am a fat womon
I can speak for myself
but what would I say to you?
Why do I think I need
to tell you how much
sugar, how much meat
I eat in a day, in a year?
Why do I think I need
to tell you how often I go swimming
or how, if my feet hurt,
it's a problem anyone can have,
fat or thin, why
do I want to tell you
the statistics about dieting
the fact that it's thin people
who suffer most from heart disease.

And why do I think
no matter what I tell you
you will you think I'm lying.
Unless I tell you I spend all my time
eating chocolate cake in front of the tv.
That I eat three chocolate cakes a day
and two six packs of coke
in between my six meals
and I get up in the middle of the night
to eat pancakes.
You'd believe that, wouldn't you?
And I remember
when they called all
fat womyn fools.

X.

I am a lucky fat womon.
If I lie in bed and have a fantasy
about eating six chocolate cakes
of being fed six chocolate cakes
by six fat womyn
who are admiring my six new rolls of flesh
I can get   pleasure from my fantasy
and know that it's resistance
to this ridiculous persistence of shame
thrown at me.
I can get up and go about my business
without too much pain,
struggle with how I eat like every womon I know—
does wheat give you arthritis,
do the chemicals they inject into apples
give us cancer in our apple juice?
How do I balance my years of anger and deprivation
with my desire to eat what's "good for me"?

How do I know, when they say it's good,
it isn't this year's medical fashion hoax,
another way to hate fat womyn?
I like to eat.
I like to feed other womyn
and be fed
when I can bear that intimacy.
I like intimacy when I can bear it —
when I can trust you.
I have appetites in my mind
that I cannot express in my body
at least not yet,
I work on it.

But I hear what's been said
when I look in the mirror
and I'll be honest
I have the words fat and ugly
paired in me.
The pairing of the words
makes me turn away faster
than what I actually see.
I touch myself and I
feel good beneath my hands
Sometimes I have lovers sometimes
they enjoy my body and enjoy me
enjoying theirs.
When I don't have lovers
I feel good beneath my hands.
This makes me a very lucky fat woman.
If I believe the evidence,
the testimony of other fat womyn,
it makes me an extraordinary fat woman
and that's a tragedy.

XI.

A very thin womon, disabled,
tells me how she spent a day crying
because she was afraid to get
on cross country skis
afraid of her own fragility,
afraid to be physical in the world.
She tells me because I would understand
and I do.
I know womyn who are fat who vomit.
I know womyn who are thin who vomit.
Womyn close to me hate their bodies,
womyn who know everything in this poem already
hate their bodies.

Womyn hate our bodies.
We have been working for justice, out of love,
in the different ways we understand it,
for years, in a hundred movements.
We have been going to twenty therapies
bodyworkers and twelve-step groups—
And remember we're lesbians
we lust for one another in our good moments
we tickle and rub
and   we   hate   our   bodies
What keeps you from understanding
what you do to me?
What did they pay you to do this to yourself?
Who does this to us?
Where is our courage?
And what happened to our resistance
to our simple stubbornness
not to let our enemy win
not to let our enemy win inside us.

only
light in the forest
fog deep over sea
width and height of redwoods
song of spider
song of leaf on leaf in the mountains
a thousand green shadows
moving

the things that heal
without thought of healing

the world that signs itself
& has no other need for speech

Some notes on the nature of the bad queen

The bad queen lived in
a cut glass palace at
the bottom of a lake.
She commanded bubbles,
and the bubbles
never had the nerve to break.

Now try to remember her seriously.
The point about the bad queen is
she is always too beautiful too exotic
too vain too arrogant too greedy
too pushy.   Too much.
Demanding and impossible to touch.

When you dream about her
you fear she is your mother
or your sister, and she will
deny you in your hour of need.

The bad queen betrays women.

She is always the Other.

She changes costume to meet
our necessity to name her
Vashti, Helen —
it's hard to remember
good queens, isn't it?
The queen has no peer.
She's alone in the palace.
She has spies who want her favor
but her lover is always a secret.

Who loves the bad queen?
The cold, the ruthless,
the isolate woman —

whose country is this?
She stares in the mirror.
No one brings her daisies
or sends postcards.
She has no living mother.
There's a rumor
she turned her daughter into a frog.
She has been initiated
into some mystery
but no one ever says how
or with whom.

You're afraid
she'll take it upon herself
to initiate you
without your consent
without telling you the rules —
she's the queen
after all.

Who would choose
to be the bad queen's lover?

Centuries have stripped her
of all ornament.
There is only the will to power
that comes across
as self-obsession.

Once she had at least
control of the women's quarters,

but the women
are decimated
hiding in separate tiny houses.

Maybe the bad queen had a vision.
Maybe she had only desire.
Maybe she was battered or tricked
into submission.
Maybe she left behind
a secret manuscript
we have yet to discover
naming every act
every choice

the passion she had
to touch
each one of us

the bright fury
with which she hungered
to illuminate her lands.

A fool for love

It's harder now, to organize,
than in my 20s.   Then
when I said I wanted to do it for lesbians
if there was a question
the question was
why do it for lesbians, who are they?
I was sure of my answer
of my love and pride
my pride in love

But now I fear
when I say I want us
who so clearly need each other
to speak every phrase of that need —
I want journeys with womyn
I can depend on, who can depend on me

I fear
the answer will be:
o that old thing

And no one wants to be a fool for love

Redwoods gutted by fire and ax
still grow
Where one redwood is destroyed
a ring of young trees sprout
redwoods have shallow roots
they need these circles
where root holds fast with root

after everything that's happened
because of everything that's happened

I want to imagine a world
in which we thrive
where difference engages us
and root holds fast with root

oakland: february 1991, 1 a.m.

Put me in mind of my harbor,
the easy romance of my luck.
The taste is bitter, the moon is frayed.
They say I know what I'm doing
but I whistle to myself:
the jig is up.

I've lived through enough wars in comfort
to know that living comfortably through wars means
nothing
is only circumstance.
Somewhere tonight there's an iraqi dyke who
believes in herself who takes what she's given
and makes do,
who loves womyn and her own power
to accomplish, to hide, to get by, to create,
to make a life she thinks her mother can't imagine
and that lesbian might be blown to bits
before I get to the end of this
page

At the start of this war Evelyn called me up
raved and grieved
all the wars she'd seen —
at seventy-nine, she can describe war after war
her family in israel   her grandchildren in danger
her heart in danger of
remembering the twentieth century
miserable egos lousy mistakes
that rage across our planet
— now I don't think the salk vaccine was worth it
the telephone, the automobile.

So this is it: I live through wars.
I live in a country that kills all over the globe and never

has a bomb dropped within its shores and I get to tell
the girls who come after

how a womon's life can be full of personal happiness,
rich with work and friendship while
human beings are vaporized with her taxes
and she she's up at 1 a.m. again
                                        watching another war

Trying to understand Rosebud[♀]

The first thing a revolutionary has to know:
                              don't get caught
They teach this
even in the boy's camps.
                    Perhaps you thought: *those wimps.*

Maybe you didn't
spend enough time
with the womyn
who add: If it's worth dying for
                     then live.
                     Avoid macho posturing.
                     Do the work.
                     Hope is patience, and belief.

            Or maybe you dismissed us: *Are those virtues?*

I'm employed by the newspaper.
I drive home through berkeley after midnight.
The night of the day you died
someone's overturned a huge garbage container
blocking a lane. On telegraph avenue
police have set up barricades, stop
every young black man for questioning.

This is it: garbage in the streets
an excuse for the police to exercise
their power, *their* beliefs.

[♀] Rosebud Denovo, a woman in her twenties, was killed by Berkeley, California, police in August 1992. She had broken into the residence of the chancellor of the university of California, armed with a machete. She was protesting the university's decision to make People's Park into volleyball courts. Everyone had been evacuated, and she was cornered in a bathroom when she was killed.

The newspapers have interviews.
Aside from your friends
who are dismissed casually

no one cares. Or they're sorry
for the chancellor, or mrs. chancellor
or innocent freshmen, this rude introduction
to the fearful circus of berkeley.

No one can imagine a woman
so full of anger and purpose
she'd go with a knife and machete
into the chancellor's house screaming:
>   no more abuse of power
>   no more hierarchy of privilege
>   there's a class war on the streets of the city
>   and you live here serene, saying
>   let them eat volleyball
>   *no more*

We read in the newspapers
you were always angry
fought school principals, police,
learned the language of pipe bombs,
lived on candy bars and pepsi.

My lover says: I can identify
with her rage —
she did what I feel inside me,
I've just been socialized out of it.

A woman who could not bear authority.
Who saw power as exploitation.
>   — it's for your own good   you'll understand someday
>   you'll have your turn
>   be a good girl   learn your place   accept —

Fuck you.
I don't have to take this.
No one should take this.
Pay attention: no one should take this.

Our compliance is imposed upon us by force.

See?

american wounds

North dakota/canadian border
by the side of the road:
a rock carved along its natural line
in the shape of a buffalo
covered with trash
shoved tight into a wire cage.

On the historical marker:
"this sacred object
was moved from its original site"

Woodpeckers

Three times since the eclipse I've seen
red-headed woodpeckers.
In the bird book with its shiny plates
there is no "red-headed woodpecker,"
the closest match is "acorn."
One morning we woke early from noise —
three perched on Linnea's house.
Acorn planters, they use
an intermediate object
to get what they need.
Each acorn they place in a branch,
under the eaves, is a seed home.
They farm for bugs, their own crop,
where first light reaches
the pitched roof in the clearing.

Today I sit alone, reading —
a womon writes "faith" "divinity."
I am studious and quiet.
Faith in what? divinity from where?
I remember grappling with this
before, alone, a child standing by a lake
or ocean — who is the queen of the sabbath?
Is there an intelligence that guides
reincarnation? Is there more
than science in the orbit
of our random planet,
so unlike the veils of hydrogen
that trail between stars?

Those are the regular questions.
We answer by our station —
a womon close to her mother
will take her mother's faith.
A wandering womon will answer

as is common among those
with whom she stays or
she will travel toward those
whose answer suits her.
She will widen whatever space she finds
according to the custom of her times.
Push a little here, interpret there,
like store bought clothes that never fit,
we make do. We wear the faith
we can afford.

Reverence, observance, deity, wonder,
awe, praise, heritage, spirit:
this impulse we hold to be
filled with the presence of the world,
and through that saturation
to lose the boundary of self
gathered up
in that-which-is-great, that-beyond-us
which still remembers our name.

The woodpecker interrupts me. Tick, thack,
tick tick until I look. Without my glasses
its margins blur. I hold still, struggle
for focus. The woodpecker walks thoughtfully
along a dead aspen reclining in a hemlock's arms,
considering each peck. I want a sharp view
but when I get back with my glasses it's gone,
only her "tick thack" somewhere in the woods.

Naturalists must wait like this, patient
in the quest. A footprint, a branch,
any sign of what they stalk and they stay,
making notes, preparing to photograph
an appearance — someone pays
for photographs, for clear plates in bird books.
Naturalists and rabbis have a lot in common.
Someone pays them to wait

for inspiration, for proofs
that there is still hope on the planet, still
nature and creation.

The rest of us are lucky if we have a little time
an occasional holiday
where we see a bird we've never seen before.
Where our questions, our mothers' questions,
have time to expand in the air
before they disappear again over the dry ridge.

Poem for the protection of my loved ones
for Tryna, going into surgery

The world turns and shivers.
I put my finger on the warm pulse
hushing up my neck I speak
into the telephone   surgery at 8:30   yes
I remember the emergency room
Does sending energy depend
on knowing the receiving terminal?
I have seen the faces of many womyn
after surgery   I know yours by heart

By heart: inside my veins where friendship
accretes   and rebuilds the body we
think is ours I find your face   with ease

If I send my energy   back   to us
walking a long redwood trail
on the oregon border eight years ago
will that energy break its barrier and find you
lying on a bed of cattails in a hospital corridor
laughing because you're safe safe:

everything heals you   the world you
thought you would never make
fills the wound with soft herbs and
lesbians are everywhere   our hands
never stop moving   even
when one of us falls or dies   we form
around her absence   clotting scabbing
fixing the skin that contains us   and tonight
I wish— the moon is just past full and I
wish on the world
I wish on our belief   on our possibility
on our enormous grief as well as our courage

to protect you   to find you here
protecting me   wherever a blade might go.

Take anything

for Dolphin

I

Experience was supposed to be our friend,
and we learn
but as we learn we get worn away.
Any smooth rock on the beach
will skip and gleam but
brought home
heaped on our table
we wonder at its dullness
the day forgotten.

She was smiling there was water
the reflection of light on water
she handed me a stone
or I picked up a stone when
I was on the beach away from her
and saw the bodies of dead birds
twisted into kelp.
I thought beach rocks
would help me remember
everything: love and mortality
the glistening of the air as I turned toward her.
Now I live alone in oakland
with a pile of stones.

II

In a city gallery we find
kelp twined into baskets by artists.
At least it finally has a use.

The city blows sand
in the eyes of our memory
stings the pleasure off our rural shores.

A day at the beach:
girls use kelp for whips
they pretend to slash each other
or they don't pretend
they do
the children wash bloody ankles in salt water.

III

But we had nights, didn't we?
Fires in a sand pit
and the girls danced for the joy of it
I walked alone
watching the moment the tide turned
feeling the pull of gravity
the slight shift of motion at sea.
Then you were there, guiding me back
to the womyn, the fire
holding out your hand
and in your hand
all your favorite stones and beads.
Take anything,
you said to me.

These things:

my heart is broken
my heart is wide open

my heart is broken
the way land is broken
after earthquake, heavy flood.
pastures still invite the eye
but lie treacherous with mud,
sinkholes, sudden fissures.
hillsides erode in graceful terraces
that threaten to slide.
the landscape's cut up
with barren inexplicable places
but still
offering shade
beneath almond trees
where womyn might rest and feast
on islands in that shattered geography
as difficult to get to
as they are dangerous to leave.

A deliberate slowing

It rained for weeks

I've seen the nature film:
where the cracked river bed floods
and a frog startled into life
bursts from mud

There are creatures that persevere
dried and patient
underground   for years

Time lapse photography
has changed our imaginations

Quick   I am kissing you
streets are wet, full
of fallen fruit blossoms   you
motion me close to your breast
the ground saturates, reservoirs fill

Then
sudden relentless quality of heat
a moment of still uncertainty
before all the small creatures
burrow backwards in their land
toward the cool, unseen place
ready to wait
a season   a generation
for cloudburst

At first pushing the pulse back hurts
but we learn
a deliberate slowing of the heart
insures survival
in the harshest loops
of our cycle

the thing we long for

the ticking is rocking away in the night
with our hearts half curdled and the moon not right
and all of the animals twitching and spry
to get their own chances for whatever lies
                                    beyond the rise

dark under fog
reflecting only the black sparks in the stream
dark at the back of the yard

and this quiet starts us baying
whenever we have no idea what we mean

there's a shape out there
a quantity
we know it   we gnash our teeth in our dreams
all elusive, and still concrete

we don't find the words
we don't find the thing though we dig in the soft sand
we've got maps in hand
marking the tree stump where it was hid
we know its circumference
its jingle   its absence of shine
its weight
                but damn if we can see her face

Blood letting♀

for Sheila Gilhooly

She could only hear the blood in her head.
She could hear it quite loudly.
Moving up there.
The doctors say it's impossible
for blood to make that sound, their
procedures are clean, electrical, convenient.
There is no blood
when these procedures are
in effect. No pain to feel.   She must
be fantasizing pain.
And that's reason enough
to wire her up again.

Nevertheless the pain is real.
She does the simple thing, cuts
her wrists deep to let the blood.
Then
everyone is afraid.

This is the wrong place to be walking
when you need to bleed.
There is proof that blood needs to be shed,
to be cupped, to be sucked, to be given up but
we do not accept this proof.

Womyn bleed to death internally,
the bones of madness
stuck in our throats too polite to scream
help me

♀Written after seeing the slideshow *Still Sane*, from the remarkable book by the same name, by Persimmon Blackbridge and Sheila Gilhooly, published by Press Gang, Vancouver, BC.

It's everywhere, not just on the wards.
Moments, days of pain that have no outlet
no ritual, not so much as a mark in our soft flesh

I have been hurt, the dream cries.
The shape of the dream itself bleeds into sleep,
until sleep is changed.
Then you may need to hit a vein.
You may need to howl through blood,
smear your body across the landscape: your room,
your job, your lover's face, someone's grave.
The monthly blood hardly satisfies
the way blood teeming from a sharp slice
in your arm might   if the occasion was right

I know what suicide is   and this
has nothing to do with it   the womon
has no desire to die

but live in ritual,
open the blood hope
where suffering
has been denied

My mother's gifts

My mother still stands in the corridor
writing letters on the institution walls
sealing pieces of plaster in envelopes
that are slow in the overseas mail reaching me
I tear them open
plaster covers the floor.
My regrets pock the dust
the way meteors attack the moon
no atmosphere to stop them.

My mother brought me to the door of the locked ward
She wanted to   touch me
        You   are my only daughter
I didn't let her   I didn't wave goodbye   I was thirteen
eleven years ago last october at midnight   I forced my
mother
away
There are certain events one always remembers.
Later on there may be other confessions
glossy and useless as the sunday comics.
                                        All these years
the only presents she sends
are sweaters:
when she travels, she remembers
her daughter lives in the north alone
She doesn't want me
to be cold.

my mother used to have that dream

We were standing in her kitchen
the kitchen of the womon who
had been my lover
I was trying to leave
She didn't want me to go
I didn't want to go
but I could see no other
way to be
She could not move toward me
she was crying
she said it wasn't that she
didn't want to, she didn't know
what stopped her
my need wasn't strange or
unreasonable to her still
she could not respond to me
unless we were having this scene
she said she dreamed she could not
move,   she opened her mouth
and no words came out
I said
my mother used to have that dream
she was standing on a beach
watching her children drowning
swept away on the surf
and she couldn't move to save them
she opened her mouth, like you,
but she could not scream

I am my mother's daughter
I am out beyond the breakers
in dangerous water
the womon on the beach
sees me go down
tangled in kelp, exhausted

or a huge wave
catches me in its break
I see her standing there
fixed   unable to swim toward me
unable to make a sound,
neither cry for help nor encouragement

I have been lost at sea
to many womyn in just this way
including my mother
one minute they are thinking
everything is well with us
and the next
I'm a ghost

What they never see is how I
surface on the other side
of the wave
paddling slowly
for another coast

We change each other

I am a womon of opaque windows
set at oblique angles
a face in each one
covered with nylon stocking or gray crepe.
You know
this image.
I close the shutters of my body
one by one
— let no light in this house
and don't poke around in my vagina either.
You refuse to take it
seriously.
Suddenly I turn a corner
in the twenty-fourth corridor
where all the windows are made
of polished black amber
and the sills are volcanic ash.
There you are
you've brought your bright red pillow
you've got your feet up against the window
and have hung your goddam plants.
Doesn't that look nice?
No   I say   get out
I may love you in meadows
but this is queer palace
no room for two.
Effortlessly you unhinge the locked blinds.
There that's better these vines need sun.
Come on now — we have to live where we can.
I start to weep
and you pull me to your breasts
with tough hands

Tell me a story

"Let's say we have a mystery guest
she has turquoise skin—"
I lie in the shallow of your armpit
waiting for the story to begin but really
I want to tell you how I lived in a turquoise house once
the only turquoise house on the block
because my mother was in the hospital and my father
had it painted as a surprise,
how shocked, aggrieved my mother was
how I wanted to be like my father,
paint a whole house in colors no one else used
for fun, for the hell of it.
I want to ask now that you've met my father
and you can see how like him I modeled myself,
witting and unwilling,
do you still love me
for my simple lesbian ingenuity?
Do you love me as one-who-comes-from-a-family
as well as for this fierce orphan independence
I take? Quick, I want to say, tell me quickly —

We were all at dinner, the two of you talking law
and I saw the way the boats moved up and down
on their moorings, the way the bay darkens as night
infuses the water
—your sex darkens sometimes that way
from a change in the atmosphere that appears
to come from underneath —
that's what I want to say: the surface can shine from
some ordinary or even horrible thing happening
and that happening, which we attribute to ourselves,
may not be ourselves at all,
but we walk around pleased with us, strut, almost,
convinced we're originals, while we
mirror our families or place,
not even having the grace of precise observation.

I am quiet and looking at you
— your sex darkening from a change in atmosphere
that seems to come from underneath...
"Comfortable?" you ask me
and I shift my weight until my face is as close
to your scent as I can make it be
cinnamon and sweat,
some dry, rusty, calming smell and the smell
of coconut oil from your neck,
"Yes," I say, "comfortable.
Tell me a story."

Carrying the Ark♀

For Susan L.

You take everything seriously.
My flesh is in your palm   your face is hot
and above me. On the couch
you are young, 15, then 25, silly, pulsing
with found love   but in bed
you age the forty desert years
want narrows your cheeks
while your fingers lengthen and you insist,
insist on repeating my fantasies until
we are chanting words, mine, yours
— more — a wail of longing and disbelief
through which we make our way
toward faith, that breathing arc faith is,
arches from precipice to ledge, my hands banding
your wrists while you shudder and wave, ark
in which the surviving remnant is carried,
the sacred words are kept.

You remember
everything that has happened since the diaspora,
the burning synagogues, the dogs of selma.
You cannot watch movies about brutality,
you must have tenderness now real
tenderness   and sex has to be this unexpected yard
marvelous with hue and bloom;
beneath the canopy
where we have stopped to rest
messages spelled in tangles by the wild hard root.

Sex has to be
your hands in that dirt   has to be

♀ The ark is the cabinet in which the torah is kept. Traveling by foot, an ark may be
carried fastened to poles which rest on the shoulders.

112

the dirt turning over, dark, reliable, origin of ritual,
our lost holidays coming back
succos, purim, pesach —
the invocation of a hunger that spreads,
joining the drifting continents
of childhood and middle-age   and you
are so serious, cupping the promise
as I cup your face —
we write over the sheets, the dirt,
the page, we turn and have at last
the secret of sex
scrolling back my skin to let you seek
your covenant in me.

Alchemy

the wizard opens her doorway.
sometimes there are flowers.
a peach would be nice.
but out of season.
anything out of season
is not in reason.
so she says.
what happens in that doorway
anyway?
I say I can see it.
the wizard doesn't say anything.
any fruit I give her
she changes
how does she change it?
well just the way I would
by eating.

great barrier reef

night diving
on the great barrier reef
sex is
to approach a sleeping fish
tenderly
to find her nook
and pull her out
press your eye to her lidless eye
stare down her knowledge
of the depth

without startling
without waking her

even my eyes become mouths

Forgetting what I'm about
your naked belly appears to me
wet from the bath
as you walk around   and I
am laying you down
with a palm on each of your sides
until full & pushed
you open
the pomegranate, the fig
got nothing on this   as
I press my face
into the hot bowels of you
and even my eyes
become mouths
to drink that juice

like paradise

your body is like paradise to me
not the stormy paradise of adam and eve
fruit hanging everywhere
and serpents steaming up the trees
this
is simpler   it
doesn't hiss
only whispers
your scent across the sheets
on occasional wednesdays
your flesh unwrapping the night
moving towards, away, towards
my hand cupping a fold of your belly
pulling me up to you before
the alarm starts its last song
this
sturdy, unmentioned time
where my eye pressed to your heart
photographs a landscape
of thick, vital womyn
a world where love
does
change everything

Bowls—A Series

for Susan Jill

The Gift

I

Containers for contexts:

Glass for childhood
Wood for what's broken & what can be grown
The pottery of our bodies
Metal that sings at our touch
Sky that holds us & comes next

Patient hours go into these shapes
and I find it's
not simply a question of creating bowls
into which I can give

but how I hold
what's come to me

I used to be hungry for the poetry
of middle and old age
what happens   what happens
when womyn take their own shape
become the body of their experience

Now I am a middle-aged woman
seeking forms that can speak for me
in their delicacy and intent

Outside acacia bend in the rain
there are glacial bowls cut into rock
there are bowls woven from
willow bark so fine and tight

they do not leak

I collect these contemplations
but their urgency frightens me
I often seek electronic consolation
Take me away
from what I know

I clasp my hands
and press my knuckles hard into my teeth
I don't like to wet my face like this

Am I cracked pottery
crizzled glass
meshed steel

        How many throws does it take
        to feel satisfied
        with the shape?

      Alone in the studio
      I paint tiny designs, teach myself intaglio
      shatter the day's work, melt the pieces down
      but gradually I name the bowls
      and give each their place

II

These are my bowls
hold them with me

All this starts
in what our own love
can & cannot carry

I realize how I may appropriate
your work   saying

you can do it this way &
if you don't want to do it this way   just
see it can be done
take heart   start to do it on your own

Too many voices tell you what to do —
if you need a way to trust your strength,
the curve of your grace holding your own gifts
if you need to know
it's up to you
what to offer and what to take
find you can be filled without glut
share without being consumed

that's yours to do and
mine only to encourage

not knowing what to give you
turning 40
I choose to give
what I know how to make

Bowls of words

Glass

We come with our fairytales complete

> glass shatters
> we cannot keep it safely in our homes
> slivers of glass pierce the heart
> glass   or ice
> the snow queen scoops the child
> who lives removed
> from the broken pieces
> of a brittle childhood

She lives where everything is danced
pretty   under a dome of glass
nothing can change the seasons of artifice

It's a story we tell about our mothers
     how our mothers
couldn't hold us   couldn't embrace
the round pliant shapes of their bodies
                              withheld

We know this story so well
we're inclined to see it everywhere
the shape of earth heaped up in mounds or
any round ornament   attracts and repels us

we feel trapped behind
walls of industrial glass

> dreaming we can see the moving crowd through our case
> but cannot reach or be reached toward
> glass so thick no voice can penetrate

>   what kind of glass is that?

A friend says   remember how they told you
it was only old glass that warps and shimmers?

Not true she said
they lie about everything
glass is liquid   all glass keeps moving
any huge plate will show the shift in motion
it's just slow
we can't measure it in days
                              This glass

                    flows into bowls
     and the bowls are carved with fantastic geometries

Hold them to the light

        We had other childhoods
            where prisms, pattern, anything etched into glass
    quickened our imagination

        We have childhoods in us still
                where the bowl of glass
                        is no trap
                but molten, glowing, a river

Wood

I

There are bowls that break.

Not always the most fragile.
Not every poem is gentle.
Some hold old bitterness and won't let go, a root
wrapping around a stone which changes its progress

The grain of wood splits
and we are never prepared for it

Old stories.   Do I hold them or spill them out?
I argue with myself.   There is no need.
No need to say where we've been, to give
the hard history along with the fancy flights of atoms?

Eight years ago we were lovers   I lived in oregon
you came to visit
the dunes, the beach, it was
cranberry festival   you stole me an opal ring
we were thieves then but
you bought yourself
a wooden bowl
myrtlewood   you loved it   I remember

I remember what did not happen to me
as if you transmitted it
        the worry in you lying in sheets across my spirit

        You say this is not my business

Eight years you've said it's not my business

> how your lover smashed the wooden bowl
> in your kitchen
> how it flew across the room and broke

This simple thing you had for yourself
This simple thing made from wood
its own elemental property
living substance made to hold
our meals, our greens

This simple thing you shared with me
meant to be sturdy, functional,
powerful and ordinary

                                        Split

& lost in the violent gesture

                          can't fuse wood back together

         We have to start again

                              from seed

II

Okay that's my version
and you're still telling me
it's not my business

so much of it had nothing to do with me
so much of it changed my life with you

            I was there   there with you
            and I am here
            throughout it   I watched everything change
and change again
                  I found an end of violence   and saw new hope
                  molded carefully, patiently on your lathe

the wood not yet able
to take the shape   you want

I know we have to find ways to live
with what's broken inside us
and I record what we can't talk about

Aren't you noble?
                you sneer at me
caught in this narrow circumference
You want to tell me everything
                 & hate it when I reflect

The root curving comes to contain
what falls into its grasp
a lens is a bowl
I collect there a mirror of rain
shaded by my own elements
still when you look
                    there's your face

III

It is possible
                to remake flesh and bone
                without science, by faith

but difficult

We are difficult womyn
so it must be our fate
to do difficult things

Plant new forests   learn the patience
of creating what we need

the strength of trees which widen in wet years
hold in drought
each to make her own grain

even as their roots cleave & collide

We will have new lumber yet
New bowls

and our same lives
going forward with both
what's broken and what's whole

Pottery

A womon can shape a bowl
out of the scattered elements of her feeling
She can invent herself
even now
after the first excitement has gone,
the revolution unwrapped, revealing
broken pots and shards
We have taken years
gluing pieces together   now
we want to start
with new direction

We have the elements inside us
a little copper, a little iron, a little hydrogen,
phosphorus, salt
we can build a kiln between our ribs
the place where the ribs spread apart
is a good place to start construction
brick upon brick of feeling

It's like that with reinventing yourself
you have to go back to the beginning
you have to mix mortar   mud   straw
you have to make the goddam bricks
you have to imagine heat so fierce it could
rearrange the shape of your pottery
you have to go down to the river banks to
get the mud
you have to find the river that someone
sang to you in a song when you were twelve
and you barely remember the words
you have to tie leaves together
to carry the mud back to your town
you have to let the wet clay

dry out the skin of your palms
while you lay your hands
around the waist of your bowl
you have to remember
to light the kiln days before
you can put your bowl   in
you have to find the phosphorus lying around
in your armpits   the dry twigs hanging out in your guts
somehow you know how to train the sun on these things
they spark   your kiln glows shudders
will it hold   will it heat
you put your bowl in
too nervous to sleep
the first bowl breaks when you open the door and the cold air
touches it   it was glowing red and now it's fragments
you have to start over
you can start over
you can do what you want to do
you just have to keep doing it
this time   you let the fire die out   the kiln cool
when you open the door
your bowl
shines at you

blue and opalescent

Metal

I hold the metal bowl over a candle flame
heat infuses the base, the rim
I cup the bowl over my face
close my eyes   and breathe

My breath fogs the shine
and I'm pleased for no reason
with the momentary print of my existence
in what will outlast me

Eight metals make a singing bowl.
There are forges in tibet and nepal
where secret elements are mixed
through huge heat   transformed
to bring in sound   through touch.

No ornament
but bowls aren't ornaments —
two sides to each of them.

We focus on what they contain
how sound or light collects
will it keep our food, our treasures, our secrets
safe   we forget
how we hold the bowl ourselves
how the outside
is a drum, or armor, or a breast
how comfortable our hands feel
stroking the contour
our fingers loose
wandering across a rounded plane

Chambers of perception
sounding experience —
we must learn
the art of holding

to make our bowls sing

Night & Sky

I

Are we held in
or dropped to this place
cupped
or thru the fingers of a careless hand
let loose
to pace and blow across the planet?

Is there a way
to fall outside the sky?

Here is the bowl
that holds you
the bowl so full
so hollow
you cannot touch its shape
nor find escape
from all these other noisy grains
which rub against you
complain & chafe

Here: the night is thick
and full of us

We love our outline in the air
and are created
by the boundaries we create

II

Our pattern is a thick
condensation of atoms

They say the universe
is different than the earth
this planet an unrepresentative sample
but we knew that, didn't we?

Outside our petty gravity
space and stars are made
of the simplest elements
what's basic, light, naive

They know this because
whatever burns shows its spectral core
what stars consume for fuel
is the clue

How did we ever get so dense?
Imagine us let loose
as hydrogen vapors   streaming
the wide cool length
between stars
                          stripped
of props
                 no more calcium
copper, lead, uranium

     becoming the
bright primordial building blocks

     a new generation

fragments
from lesbos

selections

Everyone
I suppose
must go thru
true love once but
once should be enough
to know
that as illusions go
true love is
one of
the worst
and keeps us
from our friends,
our work

Great stars sweep the sky.
It is early morning
in Kansas.
If I shook your shoulders
would the straw fall out?
Would your teeth
rattle like broken marbles
in the cave of your mouth?

Amy
I ran last night down Christopher Street
caressing the iron breasts of parking meters

you don't ask but i
can tell you anyway:

those poems weren't written
because i was afraid

you'd read them
and still wouldn't let me
touch you

Highway 99. Every time
I'm on the road
I think about you, eva.
But if the road is long enough
I think about every other
womon I've known too.

before you are gone
the wind breaks her bones
the fragile ends of the willow
yellow, cannot get sap
into the newest leaves
before you are gone
the moss, the lawn, split
fumes creak up from sewers
i choke, i do not make sense,
i might drown
in my own spit
before you are gone
hysterical on the sidewalk
there is no more talking,
only unable to believe
how deep the new mark is
where i fall, where
i know this grief
before you are gone
the water tears her hair
the webs at the river banks
cannot hold
whole cities wash out
and the dirt settles
farther and farther inland

she walks at sunset along the shore
sees the sand by light transformed to flesh
dark purple, wet folds
shudder beneath her step

give me a wide sky
the circumscribed portion baffles me
the small place
that belongs to community
rouses only
anger: no leaf
no star   ever
stood against me

let the softness enter you woman
        the wave has its soft under curl
        the oyster its valves, all the ocean
        creates her hard pearls but
        pearls have no value without
        the pulse fragrant at the base of the neck
        a cloud enters your veins
let it   even the chamber of will
        needs rain warm rain easy
        woman let me enter you again
        a different way

In Praise of Lust

the sensation that rises from our guts
and the pulse in the cunt
you can't resist
the fold in the flesh which
moistens your lips
and makes your eyes shine
your hands hunger
your belly rise and your thighs
dance against the bed, the floor

the truth is
it's needing you
that makes me want to die

it's been a long while
and the shame i feel
is not shame of need

but shame for all the times
i didn't know
what women were talking about

when they stretched
their eyes, their hands
towards me

you are far away
and i have
to stay here alone

staring into
my own hunger
which terrifies

and the all the other hungers
i encouraged
and then denied

witch moon
wild moon
moon of wild river
of incoming tides
cliff moon
moon rising
among rocky islands,
shadowed in the pines
north moon
coastal moon
moon of migrations
ninth moon
moon of the muses
of solitude
moon of vision
night moon in the inlet
moon in violet ribbons
over the wave
moon of patience
returning moon
nipple of the night
moon blessing
the lake, the sand shore
moon giving
full moon light
on the wet harbor
on strong hands
on wet thighs

the moon cups her hand to hold
the black breast of the sky
fog hides them in their passion
as they circle the night

small apple leaf that winces & grins
lately she has left my bed

lately she has gone downstairs
i am not sure in what spirit but
it does no good to ask these things

jelly in the hammock
red lights thru clouds that
bandage the sun

they are all different ones –
greenest riddle that's asked the blood

with her drunkest eyes   she would like to see
                the moon   keep straight   ahead of her
            as the road turns
            the trees, her eyes
                            not to know
                            more
                            than   she is a woman alone
                                and in trouble
                                she is a woman alone
                                and glad of it
        her eye peeling across craters
                rocking in life
                    she would / like
                                to be able to be
                                that way again
                                passing thru town
                                without destinations
                                without so many enemies
                    / or   so many friends

Rose the Dyke♀

Rose
tattooed her arms with
crayons
at the age of
twenty
and told me about
her "old lady"
whom one night
I met.
She was 17, drinking scotch
in pink baby dolls.
I was wearing
my black dress.
The one
my mother bought me
for the casinos.

♀ I was 18 when this happened. It was 1969, in Chicago; until I went to Rose's apartment, I
believed by "old lady" she meant her mother.

do you come from this country?

where the womyn grow twice on one stalk
mouth to mouth

one praising, saying soft now easy kid   you've
been here before it's familiar let up you can
care about yourself take the power in you   serious
rest in your strength accomplishments be comforted

and the other mouth
                              a curse pressed again
                              payments & debt
              its echo, whines, scorn, fear   bitterness

              tangled   into the first
                                        like the mouths of
                                        lovers

who might kiss themselves to death

her arm dangles along the shelf of my sleep
windows of morning
summer stretches her limbs,
our bodies:
        new shores beneath great sheets

outside of flagstaff, arizona, at dawn:

highway!
lamplight —
for those of us who've tracked the night
and suckled at its claws
venus in the east
frost on the hanging bough
great limb of cloud

       moon stalking:
          / they slid
           towards blood
           new hand
           made of silk

what does she want?

    fingers that are empty along the edge of wind
    the black iris, the black orchid

        no there is no such thing

i want the thing that always is not
that is other, that is gone

or else the cold hard type
each character cast in lead
fragile, easily smashed in the press

    the smell of iris, the orchid
    in ink
    that fragment

which intoxicates
which sends out hope to rifle the type case

and never ends the line

i'll put it
  another way:
                loving you
        makes my muscles dance around
              on my bones

                        on our love bed i imagine
                        the irises you'll bring
                        deep mouths opening
                        all night long

but
i love you most
in bed:

your hands
are like my hands
when i masturbate

        near troutdale i should have
        pulled your breasts from the blouse
        rubbed them against my cheeks like peaches,
        like apples, smelled the earth of each

or scorpions you drummed in the night dessert
of the silent, giant Navajo land   you

let your hair grow tangled
dance all night in the city
climb the narrow mountain pass
steady me with your hand
go on   deeper   into the caves
the tropic reef waters
wade into the swamps calling
the animals to you
athlete of dawn   i
am loving this

this shaking breath
womon
come to me when the moon is waxing

everything you do is tall and ample

the mountain field opens with the width of her boughs
above the lake, mounds covered with snow
the world echoes us
there is no news of the city
i put my hands on your hips
and move them
the flesh is a fountain
that sings what is best to us
breaking from rock underground
you have given me
the first secrets of your shuddering
i have come to you with mine
swelling enfolding unafraid
to travel exposed
we go down
that deep path
where the light and water   shine

twenty miles from Mesa Verde
i took you up a dark stairway,
not strong enough to carry

what's best
are those moments between
when she has left
and comes again
soon
and you are
drinking cold beer alone

i light the candle of drunkness
above your portrait
wax drops on your face
scorches it
i press a thumb to that softness
and leave my mark

thick against the screen
wetting the window, wetting the sill
wet knapsack and still coming
silence as it adorns me
leaves me watchful
watching how calm comes this year
our birth together
our wet october
stretching the dark membranes
mulch, sand, muscle,   open
open   rain   fertile

          some   one
                              Must
  someone does
              eat the sky with her hands

this is my vagina's song
oh it won't be long now
it won't be long
before i grin and smile at you
before i take off
tap dancing
free at last
from all the underwear
of my beneath-the-sheets past
              oh my vagina sings
and thumps itself in melody
sweet sweet fingers
gentle hands
rub and caress
it won't be long now
it won't be long
before she grows green shoots
into scarlet runnerbeans
crops of the dawn
when my vagina's free

sea underwind has
stretch marks
like the breasts & stomachs
of new womyn

Linda At Eight

      round hill.   open forest.   this
fragile thing.   streaks across a cold moon.
the young salmon arching.   she dances, dances
at the edge of the wave.   tree stump in purple
sand.   berries just beyond reach in the clearing.
a weasel at the river bank. her face is small
and clear beside the night. day break on
fossil ledge. this fragile thing. the

promise we cannot name.   the promise we keep.

flight of ravens
across the marsh at the edge of land
so many wings span the stars
she speaks my name
the marsh has noises that wash
beside our bodies
all night   all night long
a meteor comes up among black clouds
smearing the sky with orange
her lips go down

she is awake in the sunrise
she speaks my name
a new sound among the reeds,
the low wind on shore
she places her hand on my arm
on the hot side of my face
the story of this love goes on
as they travel behind the borders
as they make camp by the water

we have been sent to wake you
the voice of the golden throated ones,
the marsh birds over head
all along

diving,   i kiss and/kiss and/ kiss
        and/& kiss
        kiss/and kiss
                       :underneath
you are coral
          live   red   coral

i brush the windchimes with my shoulders
    the polished agates sing

and your face is smiling   your
    hands are
        on my flesh again

Whale Poem 2:   **For She Who Still Thrives**

i do not hear them
but i can imagine
i know they're there
and how the long cool night is
underwater
the light from the stars
is smaller
but the moon
the moon is shining
through the ocean
she lifts her head
and the moon collects
in rocking drops
across her brow
then she sings again
i do not hear her
but i can imagine
in the dark
i see the waters
glide and shadow
beyond the sandbar

my love

is amber
when pain leaves her
a flare of hot light
illuminates the air
fuses
the million volumes of space
there
is a color beneath
the stunning embers
that circle her face
a health
a challenge
drawing my love
through the boundaries
with
her ragged golden eyes

my love is copper

    she conducts electricity

    and becomes the current

her hands are musician's hands

and her muscles are the muscles
of a working mechanic

she makes   art
    from winding around
    and through   sparks

she knows   where   to touch them

        my love
                is rose

    she is the shadow of wine
        on white cloth

        many rainbowed refractions   growing
            around her

      shaft of light   within   shaft of light

        turning   changing

            as touch   or wind
            shakes the wineglass

the flesh is a sweet river
no the flesh is a fountain
the flesh becomes a ream of paper
the flesh is breasts that come as mountains
the flesh has been hidden in caves
under limestone under mortar
bricked in in tenements
the flesh as slave labors
the flesh sweats
the flesh stinks
the flesh is dark against the stars
the flesh is rosy from the bath
red hot
the flesh is its own amusement park
its own nature trail
without guidebooks or tickets
the flesh is the one thing you grab in handfuls
suck from the nipple or the crease in the knee
old flesh is wrinkled   smooth it
the flesh is silk
it's sandpaper   it's its own disease
it is the dream of breeze on the desert
it is the curve of the ocean
as her arm brushes your cheek
the flesh gives madness
the flesh gives ease
the flesh is rich and fat
the flesh is greased
the flesh is strong
it stretches   it lasts
the flesh is a symphony
of sparrows and crickets

african drums   greek choruses
the flesh is
the flesh is
the flesh is living
as long as she breathes

if i put my hand on your belly and my cheek
along your fat side
if i put my mouth around your nipple   and held by breath
waiting to die
if i learned in that place instead to live   to swell
enjoy and accept
then that is what i have of you in me   even
this far from the city   where
those words were said

with its howl, its seas, its
great upheavals   the world
survives us

                                              still we
think our kiss
can change it

and does

They Will Know Me
By My Teeth

selections

THEY WILL KNOW ME BY MY TEETH

ELANA DYKEWOMAN

In the Jewelry Room
of the Egyptian Collection

where everything was precise
it was woman's

then cowrie shells, in silver, in gold,
folding lips
decorated her waist

the ring where the naked woman
stands beside she who is clothes
and at their hips   crowned snakes
ovary crowns, moon crowns,
their snake bodies entwining

all these she made
all these were taken from her

the jewelry she wore in life
the jewelry that was placed upon her body
on the embalming incision
where they lay the hawk girdle
the jewelry of death

place your hands on me

the seweret bead was placed at the throat of the mummy
the collars, the armlettes, the hawk girdle,
the isis girdle, its beaded ribbons
ripping against the centuries of dust
where she had waited for us

place your hands on the hollow where my pulse beats

the jewelry she wore in life
the cowrie, the seeds
rosettes, circlettes, lotus, acacia

she remembers how she spoke
she speaks:

place your hands on the lips
of the   living   bead

What Can I Ask

It tends to go so wrong
never a woman as strong
as I want them
as brave
– and the brave ones frighten me

What can we ask from each other?

Anytime
ask me a favor
give the favor of this dance
give me the favor of your hand
give me the favor of your faith

What can we ask

Clean up after yourself and don't cost me any money
it's hard enough to take care of me
and feed the dog

And I don't like to be called honey
and ask me out to dinner sometime
and let me trace the smile at the corner of your mouth
let me take photographs of your naked body
and let us rub our bodies together
hold me when I start crying
whisper into my ear that we
will live to see the revolution
stay with me
and never say you want to leave
and give me back the poems I've written for two years

And give me the favor of your faith

What can we ask from each other

Be strong enough to be an army
never hand over your power
never go someplace I'm not invited
never act without a reason
think of all the implications
remember to be a comparative shopper
we don't have enough money for guns
we don't have enough money for printing presses
no cash for parks, for children
don't go to the movies
give us your money
don't publish with macmillan
give us your money

What can we ask from each other

Think about the women who have always had less
try not to hate the women with more, reason with them
let us progress to the places reason can take us
it may be useless but

Any woman must answer

If we ask enough from her
if we don't go away

Will you come with me asking

Will you know what to say
will you listen to me beside you
will you tell me stories in the morning
will you bring me a glass of orange juice
will you cherish my body for its weakness and will
for its own shape

for the voice that speaks from it
will you leave me alone now
will you come when I call you
will you hold me to your breast, to the nipple
when I come at five in the morning weeping

What can I ask you

Will you change it with me so that no one comes
at five in the morning weeping
unless they want to
unless weeping tickles them

The weeping has ceased tickling me

New England Cemetery

Carved into branches some rocks shine.
Jade shines, and purple quartz.
Newspapers shine full of headlines,
these skulls shine beneath the corpse.

It's luxury the dead indulge in –

                                        Narcissa and Polly,
                                        the deacon's wife.

        Keeping it hushed
        with the handmade lace:
        what their lives were like.

                November air   sweet moss old stone
                exact the price
                of married silence.

What luxury now
to lie stopped in the country by crooked rows.
No longer shrews or virgins
their chipped names
                          rise and fall in relief
                  as the breath of women left alone.

        Daughters free
        for the first time
        to caress their mothers' bones,
        three generations wide and deep.
        No immigrant secrets left,
        their bibles shut
        & all the children tucked in:
                                  Narcissa and Polly
                                  lie back with a laugh

                                reflecting the elements.

Essay:
The ex-patriot and her name⚲

But in being faceless unmentionable nameless lesbians ... in being unable to find catch words in newspapers or the books we read in our dormitories, for that, for what that meant, women loving women—in that we could have no fads. That was where some of us began our resistance, learned to change ... who we thought we were doomed to be into who we are. Tough, strong, proud: free women.[1]

Names define reality. As soon as I heard the word "lesbian," I knew I was one. As soon as I grasped that people could call themselves writers, I started calling myself a poet. In 1975, I changed my name from Nachman to Dykewomon, and started publishing for womyn only.[2]

These are difficult realities. I struggle with the sense of isolation my choices contain while living a full (crowded) life in a field of extraordinary and loving dykes. I admire, learn from, talk to, engage with many other lesbian writers at the same time that I feel typed as the "lunatic fringe" for wanting lesbians to cast their lot (mate-

---

⚲ *InVersions: Writings by Dykes, Queers & Lesbians,* edited by Betsy Warland (Vancouver: Press Gang Publishers, 1991): 155-164.

1 *Riverfinger Women* (Plainfield, VT: Daughters, Inc., 1974): 15-16.

2 In the late 1960s, I started getting published in college journals and the straight alternative press. Since 1974, I have published a novel (*Riverfinger Women*), a book of short stories and poems (*They Will Know Me By My Teeth*), a book of poetry (*fragments from lesbos*), essays, poems, and short stories in anthologies (including *Nice Jewish Girls, Shadow on a Tightrope, Naming the Waves*), and in the feminist and lesbian press. Since 1987, I've been the editor of *Sinister Wisdom*, a journal for the lesbian imagination in the arts in politics founded in 1976.

rial as well as emotional) with other lesbians. The tension between my present realities—the misunderstood, cranky, exiled writer versus the active, happy cultural worker enfolded in her community— gnaws at me.

We were standing there sharpening the axes that would bring down our father's trees. We were pulling our mothers from their houses, we were talking to each other, we were devising witch dances where all the women of all the races and all the classes were going to dance in the cleared spaces hidden in the New England trees, we were going to teach each other all the steps and movements of the supple belly and the ways to use our breasts and many were coming together, and the axes were taken from us. How?[3]

It's the sensation of ineffectiveness that's the most frustrating. Like the generations before us, when we were in our twenties, we thought we were going to change the world. Unlike the generations before us, we also thought we were going to change the word—that changing the word would be our instrument for changing the world. We were going to change the word "woman." From woman to women, from women to womyn (wimmin), from womyn to lesbian, from lesbian to dyke to amazon, from outsider to compañera, from competitor to sister. We worked hard, we had some success (perhaps we never agreed to go far enough, to disappear words like "marriage" and suspend the use of the word "love").[4]

I believe the individual lives of many womyn and lesbians have been changed by what I and other lesbians (of all political persuasions) have done, but it's hard to see where the aggregate effect of

3 "They Will Know Me By My Teeth," *They Will Know Me By My Teeth*, (Northampton, MA: Megaera Press, 1976): 48.

4 "Why 'love' when lesbians are trying to reclaim it for ourselves?" my friend SJ asks me. "Think how we might feel about each other if we didn't always have to call it by the same word that's in every song on the radio, and couldn't say 'I love red sneakers' or 'I just love a good cry.' We might find other directions for our thoughts, new ways to act towards each other," I say. "Alright," she says, "but womyn aren't going to know what you mean."

that work exists in the world. And our new words, where they still survive, when they can't be co-opted, have often been diminished to "side-issues" or to cute/eccentric personal preferences.

ooo

I was locked up in 1962 at the age of thirteen—a queer, fat, suicidal child. I looked around the wards. I could only think of one way to transcend a life that offered either marriage or chronic institutionalization: to be a writer. Writers, I thought, might not have to be "women," are not necessarily "sane."[5]

But by the time I was in my twenties, I was grieved by my doubt that a Jewish lesbian could ever be taken seriously by the *New York Times Book Review*. I must have been twenty-five or twenty-six when my novel, *Riverfinger Women*, was published by Daughters, Inc., one of the first feminist/lesbian publishing houses. Daughters took out a full-page ad in the *New York Times Book Review*, in which only the description of *Riverfinger Women* contained the word "lesbian," despite *Rubyfruit Jungle*'s appearance in the same ad. I decided if I could make it into the *Times* that way, it was too easy. So I changed my name to Dykewomon.

Why I really changed my name to Dykewomon: it was the mid-1970s, everyone was changing their names, I liked my first name fine, but my last name connected me too directly to the long male Hasidic tradition, to a huge extended patriarchal first-generation US Jewish family from which I wanted out.[6]

And I was afraid of something. I was knee-deep in the hustle writers play, waist-deep in ego. Under the pseudonym s.p. wonder, my poems were getting published in various alternative and college magazines. I knew a small group of avant-garde writers and gay guys in the arts who knew others, who had connections in New York. A couple of straight men in a small Berkshire, MA, press wanted to publish a book of my poems. I was living on Rainbow Grease Farm with straight people who loved me, who lent me their Land Rover

5 For both theoretical and personal reflections on this experience, see *Sinister Wisdom #36: Surviving Psychiatric Assault & Creating Emotional Well-Being in Our Communities*, Winter 1988/89.
6 If I had it to do over again, I would choose a name more easily identified as Jewish.

to go to Northampton, where I found the women's movement and later, when I was living with lesbians, co-founded Lesbian Gardens (a lesbian-only loft space that was a political and cultural focal point in the mid-1970s).

Somewhere in the midst of the antiwar, civil rights, women's and lesbian movements, I started to question the value of identifying as "the outsider." Of course, these movements provided a cultural space where, for the first time in my life, I didn't *have* to be an outsider. I began to feel that "being a writer" was removed from daily life, from the ordinary and essential life of womyn, in a hollow and destructive way. You either had to choose a set of values tied to male institutions—academia and capitalist publishing—or you had to choose community. If you wanted to get reviewed in the *New York Times*, you had to write for the *New York Times*. No two ways about it—you'd have to cozy up to their perspectives, their understanding of vital writing (almost always translated as virile writing).

> *I lay in bed next to a woman who was going away from me, to live in Israel. I said. The only thing left for me is to become famous. She was revolted. She turned from me in bed. Certainly when everyone turns from you in bed there is only one thing left to do. That is to become famous.*[7]

The pursuit of that recognition struck me first as the pursuit of privilege, and second, as the pursuit of male approval. So I changed my name, hoping to keep myself honest. I changed my name so I would be in a constant state of self-examination about my motives in writing, so I would have to write as a member of the community in which I placed my heart and cunt, as a participant with a specific talent.

I have an analysis of capitalism (how it crushes us), of what happens when writers enter a male market economy, of sexual and racial politics—who gets to speak and for whom and when and why. I have an analysis of ego as motivation, and I long for my motivations to be somehow divorced from my ego. After all, I have

---

7 "Certain Scarcities," *They Will Know Me By My Teeth*, (Northampton, MA: Megaera Press, 1976): 13.

a state-made ego, that north american sense of individual entitle-ment: I could win the lottery, I could be rich and famous, I could have a best-seller. I long to never wish again for a best-seller; I hope to be able to write for another twenty or forty years, but I have little hope of being able to support myself as a writer.

Writing may be a question of what you name yourself, but publishing is a social contract. Wanting to publish for womyn- or lesbians-only, for instance, is a violation of our common beliefs about the social contract between writer and audience. The most commonly held belief is that the printed word no longer "belongs" to the writer, but to the "public," to "the ages." The writer who be-lieves that controlling context is as important and political as con-tent is considered by many as foolishly utopian at best, more often, as a self-important scold.

Wanting to publish for womyn-only and read for lesbians-only, my intentions are threefold:

- to give, open-heartedly as I can, the gift of attention. Writing and reading aloud are the most intimate things I do in life, after making love. I want that intimacy to carry over, I want to always write with my whole body, my full mind; I want to live in a lesbian context where we expect that from each other. Wanting to have that context means wanting to create it, to live in the creative process of encouraging lesbians to attend to each other.
- to insist that we have communications we need to protect, that we may be endangered individually and collectively when men read what we write; and that we undermine our strength when we disguise our messages so we will be safe if men do read them.
- to encourage lesbian network building, to encourage lesbians to understand that we need each other for economic as well as cultural survival, that we need to buy from and trade with each other to create a lesbian economic power base.

Those intentions haven't changed. I want to keep making those choices, yet it often feels like saying: I choose to walk the streets of a lesbian village on the moon—they're choices without a real location. If, for instance, you studied to be a carpenter in order to build homes and communal structures in lesbian villages, only to find there are no lesbian villages being built, you must still work, and find ways to make your work meaningful to you.

I struggle with this—I make compromises. I stop insisting that the books I'm published in be for women-only. I allow, with discomfort, that my work be included in anthologies published by some small male-owned presses (like Crossing or Beacon). I edit *Sinister Wisdom* knowing that some men read it (although I did delete the guy whose address was the state department). I don't always require that readings I do be advertised as "for lesbians-only," though I continue to insist on reading to womyn-only audiences.

> *We were delighted to speak of passion and hatred. We went on forever, looking into it, trying to lay new plans, finding ways we could use our passion and hatred as strengths, tools, shields, spears, and not get garroted with them, as we have in the past. As passion dims, resolve must stay.*[8]

Certainly I want my work to move and reach as many lesbians as it can. The great lesbian network of the 1970s never really exercised its potential economic power. Most lesbians don't seem willing to buy books or journals marked "for womyn-only" (where *Riverfinger Women* sold over 13,000 copies in three years, it took eight years to sell 3,000 copies of *They Will Know Me By My Teeth*, marked "womyn-only," to the same audience). Women's bookstores usually don't want to deal with womyn-only books. Most other writers think writing "for women-only" cuts you off not only from the possibility of livelihood[9] but from your intended audience and "the real world."

---

8 "They Will Know Me By My Teeth," *Teeth*, 46.

9 I can only think of five or six lesbians alive who have (maybe) lived for as much as a year from having their own out-lesbian work (not anthologies) published. But livelihood as a writer includes being able to get a job teaching, getting speaking engagements, writing book reviews and other magazine pieces, getting grants and acceptances at writers' colonies. All of these things depend, to some degree, at some point, on being able to please a man, to turn your attention to men and to include men in your social and political framework. To want to work only for womyn (here I don't mean publishing only for/with womyn, but simply wanting all your creative attention and effort to be directed towards womyn—let alone lesbians) means you are effectively stopped from making a living in any of these ways. The interesting thing is that this desire, to want to put all your most intimate, thoughtful, and loving energy into womyn, has been so suspect among lesbians. As if admitting to that desire constituted a threat to under-

I live every day in "the real world"—I've made my living as a secretary, administrative assistant, printer, typesetter. When I am able to work for lesbians, it's a wonderful thing—not a privilege or a luxury, but a rare essential—that gives my life substance and meaning.

Right now I work four days a week, eight months a year as a type-setter, and between fifteen and forty hours a week on *Sinister Wisdom*. I have friends and a lover, and I try to keep writing. It would be a lot easier to keep writing and editing if 1,000 (only 1,000) more lesbians subscribed to *Sinister Wisdom*. Not just because I could quit being a typesetter, but because it would create more resources, more hope. I want to see lesbians continue the conversations we start at music festivals and conferences, more lesbians engaged in creating lesbian space.

> *think of all the implications*
> *remember to be a comparative shopper*
> *we don't have enough money for guns*
> *we don't have enough money for printing presses*
> *no cash for parks, for children*
> *don't go to the movies*
> *give us your money*
> *don't publish with macmillan*
> *give us your money*
> *What can we ask from each other*[10]

Lesbian and womyn's space has always been difficult to get, harder to maintain, always subject to intense questioning. The "humanist" trend of the 1980s continues to enforce heterosexual values even in queer nation, where the unwritten rule is boys and girls

standing the dynamics of race and class; as if one (or fifty) lesbians having that desire threatened the whole fabric of coalition politics. There must be millions of men (including "radical" and "sensitive" men) who go through life doing everything they do for the benefit of themselves and other men, and if a womon should benefit, it's incidental. But that a lesbian should want to make a living working for and with lesbians somehow threatens the whole structure of society from the Right to the radical Left, and consequently, rarely happens.

10 "What Can I Ask," *They Will Know Me By My Teeth*, (Northampton, MA: Megaera Press, 1976): 63.

have to play together as if we are all equals now, and the subordi-
nate must not question the values of the dominant; must not, in
fact, let on they realize that dominant groups still exist. For instance,
early in 1990, *Out/Look* magazine staged a lesbian and gay writers
conference in San Francisco and invited me to speak on a panel. I
declined when I found out there would be no lesbian-/womon-only
space allowed at the conference ("You can caucus in a restaurant if
you want," one organizer said). It's incredibly frustrating to be back
at square one; to have to say again: womyn have different expe-
riences in life than men; lesbians have different experiences than
gay men; we have different concerns and whole other languages
that come from our differences, and we need our own spaces to (at
least) consolidate our own political power and develop/explore our
sense of identity.

We need our own senses of identity. We lesbians, we do. We
need our own racial/cultural affinity groups in which to develop
trust, culture, identity, language, economic and psychological
survival strategy. Latina/Chicana, African, Native, Asian, Jewish,
ethnic, working class, fat, old, young, disabled dykes need our
own groups. Then we need larger groups—lesbian conferences,
lesbian buildings, health care, monetary systems, agriculture,
publishing—in which to work together, learn from each other,
have a base from which we can do anything that strikes us as im-
portant in life. Without our own bases, we will always get co-opted.
Capitalism seduces us from the Right; humanism seduces us from
the Left. It makes sense to me that we should want to control the
context of our work/communities as well as their content. To
start with "your own" and move outwards is to have a wide vision
grounded in self-respect.[11]

In the real world, I've made choices I can live with, that I'm glad
to keep making. Writing for womyn and lesbians is a clear, political,
and pleasurable choice. What's hard in my choice is (only) what
was hard twenty years ago: the world is so geared towards men
we often don't notice what we lack in terms of attention. But les-

---

11 I realize lesbians are often faced with difficult decisions in defining who, exactly, is
"their own," and I don't mean to minimize the potential pain in our choices. I do think
that the more choices we have and validate for each other, the more connection
between us is possible.

bians keep talking to each other, keep changing each other's lives and minds. Sometimes I look at the immensity of the forces ranged against us and am amazed at our persistence. We keep coming back to each other with new words and fresh juice.

I complain, but the more I think about what I'm doing in life, as a lesbian and a writer, the happier I feel. I want to share this happiness. I'm lucky to be in this struggle, listening to what other lesbians say and write, re-evaluating my own motives and analyses. I am full of experience and reflection, of questions and answers, of work to do.

Sometimes when I'm alone at night, I look at my bookshelves, the piles of my and other lesbians' manuscripts that live in my rooms, and I have the sensation of being rocked in the hammock of lesbian words. The difficulties, the pleasures, the endless arguments and conversation, the voices of womyn who have died and young dykes just starting, becomes a humming that infuses me with wonder and satisfaction. And there's always the possibility that our words are working out there:

> i thought i saw for a second a letter from the other alphabet ... the one i secretly dream i am participating in making... one flaming new letter... all of us who make the new letters from the language of our lives, from the honesty, howl and longing that rise up from us — we will recognize these letters instantly — begin to be able to communicate with them — in a language which, when it is drawn, changes the mind, and when it is spoken, changes the world.[12]

12 "Journal Entry," *For Lesbians Only: A Separatist Anthology* (London: Onlywomen Press, 1988): 548.

Afterword:
Wimmin, Words, and Wisdom:
Elana Dykewomon and Communities of Lesbian Readers

Generations of lesbians have found themselves reflected in the pages of Elana Dykewomon's novels since Daughters Publishing Company Inc. first published *Riverfinger Woman* in 1974. Dykewomon's powerful debut was followed by two other novels, *Beyond the Pale*, originally published by Press Gang in 1997, and *Risk*, published by Bywater Books in 2009. This work, in conjunction with her collection of short stories, *Moon Creed Road* (Spinsters Ink, 2003), establish Dykewomon as an important novelist— and as a writer who engages lesbian experience and sensibility. While Dykewomon's novels now enjoy new audiences through reissues from lesbian publishers and as e-books, finding her poetry has been more difficult, until now. *What Can I Ask: New and Selected Poems* returns Dykewomon's poetry to print for contemporary readers to discover her powerful poetic voice.

What Can I Ask gathers poems from across the three collections of Dykewomon's published poetry. Poems from Dykewomon's book, *They Will Know Me By My Teeth* (Megaera, 1976), which included both poems and short stories, are in *What Can I Ask*. Most of the poems from *Fragments from Lesbos* (Diaspora Distribution 1981) are gathered in these pages as are a selection of poems from Dykewomon's earlier selected poems, *Nothing Will Be As Sweet As the Taste* (Onlywomen Press, 1995). In addition, *What Can I Ask* includes a generous selection of Dykewomon's new poems written during the past twenty years.

In these pages, readers discover the tenderness, passion, and commitment of Dykewomon for lesbians and lesbian communities. *What Can I Ask* is a collection that affirms Dykewomon's importance as a poet in the US tradition, and it is a collection that conveys Dykewomon's significance in lesbian literary communities. Dykewomon is a polymath who fulfilled her early promise as a literary artist by amassing a prodigious collection of work. Dykewomon is a novelist who writes stories where lesbians can see our lives reflected on the page, but she is not only a novelist. She is a poet who renders lesbian sensuality visible and lends language to lesbian intimacy and affection, but she is not only a poet. Dykewomon is a cultural worker who throughout her life has built lesbian communities—political, literary, cultural, and communal. *What Can I Ask* celebrates all of these aspects of Dykewomon's work.

When I first read *Fragments from Lesbos*, which has largely been out of the public eye for the past twenty years, I was struck by the intimacy that Dykewomon conveys among women in the poems. Certainly, part of this intimacy is sensuality and open representations of lesbian sexuality. In "Carnal Knowledge," Dykewomon writes, "my mouth was full of her lips, and I was shaking with five pleasures at once." In another poem in *Fragments*, Dykewomon discloses,

> *On our love bed I imagine*
> *the irises you will bring*
> *deep mouths opening*
> *all night long*

This configuration of lesbian erotic imagery—linking flowers with vulvas and mouths with long nights of lovemaking—now may seem a stereotypical trope, but when Dykewomon was writing in the 1970s, she was shattering taboos, expressing lesbian sex and sexuality explicitly in poetry. For me as a reader, it is still magically transcendent poetry. Yet, for Dykewomon, lesbian sexuality is not all genitalia and flowers. She engages the full body in her portrayals of lesbian lust and desire. In another poem, Dykewomon writes,

> *i put my hands on your hips*
> *and move them*
> *the flesh is a fountain*
> *that sings what is best to us*

By linking singing with touching and water, Dykewomon re-
minds readers that sexuality and sensuality appeal to the full range
of our senses. Thus, one important element of Dykewomon's work
is the portrayal of lesbian sexuality in complex, multifaceted ways.

Equally important is Dykewomon's visions for women's com-
munities. She moves easily between individual relationships with
women and more universal claims:

> Highway 99. Every time
> I'm on the road
> I think about you, eva.
> but if the road is long enough
> I think about every other
> womon I've known too.

This poem explains part of what I think Dykewomon wants
readers to take from her work: an opportunity to think about
"every other womon" we have known and to be enriched and
changed by those moments of reflection. Dykewomon's poetry
generates a sense of community and of communal involvement
and engagement. She wants us to understand and celebrate not
only what it means to be a lesbian but also what it means to be a
lesbian with other lesbians. For Dykewomon, in communal settings
the power of women crests. In all of her creative work, Dykewomon
envisions a world where lesbians work together creating worlds
that refuse and resist patriarchy, racism, and imperialism while si-
multaneously celebrating friendships, camaraderie, righteousness,
and justice. This broad vision includes a critique of a coupled dyads:

> True love is
> one of the worst
> and keeps us
> from our friends,
> our work

Dykewomon wants something greater than true love for each
of us as readers: she wants us to have friends and work that are
meaningful and sustaining. This is a loving gesture, a gesture that

reveals the generosity of Dykewomon and the powerful vision that energizes and infuses her creative work.

Dykewomon's vision for women and the possibilities our lives could contain shaped her practice of lesbian separatism. Shortly after *Riverfinger Woman*, Dykewomon changed her surname and engaged in defining and elaborating the practices of lesbian separatism. By the time she published *They Will Know Me By My Teeth* in 1976, she included this statement next to the price: "To Be Sold To And Shared With Women Only." This simple line, as assertion of the possibility of engaging in a woman-only economy and working with women only, elicited all manner of reactions. Bookstores and distributors wondered how to fulfill this request; individuals wondered about the significance and sincerity of the statement. These words challenged people to think and consider all modes of practice in their lives. Dykewomon discovered lesbian separatism was a powerful interruptor; it was a vision, an ideal, and a practice that simultaneously challenged the current regime and created new possibilities. As her work continued to develop (she was only twenty-seven when *Teeth* was published), Dykewomon continued to focus on lesbians exclusively situating her work as "for womyn-only and for lesbians-only."

Separatism shaped Dykewomon's creative output and her cultural work over the next decades. In addition to her own creative work, from 1980 until 1984, Dykewomon operated Diaspora Distribution, a lesbian separatist distribution company that handled books and other lesbian-made products, with Dolphin Waletzky. Diaspora Distribution employed the ethos of "for womyn-only," crafting new imaginative possibilities for lesbians focused on creating objects for other lesbians. From 1987 until 1994, she edited *Sinister Wisdom*. As the editor of *Sinister Wisdom*, Dykewomon continued to nurture lesbian imagination and lesbian consciousness.

Reflecting on separatism in 1991, Dykewomon explained that lesbian separatism as expressed through publishing was an opportunity "to give, openheartedly as I can, the gift of attention," to insist that women's communication is more honest and more open if it is for women only, and "to encourage lesbian network building, to encourage lesbians to understand that we need each other for economic as well as cultural survival, that we need to buy from and trade with each other to create a lesbian economic power base."[1] Twenty-five years later, lesbian separatism, often maligned and marginalized, remains worthy of consideration and thoughtful discussion. The spaces for these discussions, however, become fewer, more fleeting. In 2011, in a dialogue with Jyl Lynn Felman, Dykewomon noted that she identifies "as a radical Jewish dyke." Recognizing the flashpoint that lesbian separatism has become, Dykewomon explains that for her today separatism means holding a "radical analysis of power relations."[2] She also reflected, "Now I think revolution—deep structural change that will overthrow hierarchic power patterns—isn't something I'll live to see."[3] I hold on to willful naiveté; I hope that she is wrong—and that *What Can I Ask* will remind us of the positive and powerful contributions of lesbian separatism.

The impulse to write is an impulse to reach a community, to have a conversation with people. Dykewomon's editorship at *Sinister Wisdom* exemplifies her reach for communities of women. Dykewomon edited *Sinister Wisdom* from 1987 through 1994; between 1991 through 1994, she co-edited *Sinister Wisdom* with Caryatis Cardea. During the eight years of her editorial and organizational leadership, Dykewomon brought together communities of writers, readers, volunteers, and literary activists to produce the journal. She published issues on the topics of class, race, resistance, and religion. She worked with women to create "The 15th Anniversary Retrospective" of *Sinister Wisdom*, published in the summer of 1991 and gathering some of the most influential pieces published to date. Each issue that Dykewomon published demonstrates care and commitment to lesbians, to lesbian literature, and to lesbian ideas. On every page of every issue that Dykewomon published is evidence of her love for and belief in lesbians. On January 1, 1995, Dykewomon continued the tradition established by the founders

1 Elana Dykewomon, "The Ex-patriot and Her Name," *InVersions: Writings by Dykes, Queers & Lesbians*, edited by Betsy Warland (Vancouver: Press Gang Publishers, 1991): 159.

2 Elana Dykewomon and Jyl Lynn Felman, "Forward and Backward: Jewish Lesbian Writers," *Bridges*, vol. 16, no. 1 (Spring 2011): 230.

3 Ibid., 231.

of *Sinister Wisdom*, Harriet Desmoines and Catherine Nicholson, and gave *Sinister Wisdom* to three new editors-publishers, Akiba Onada-Sikwoia, Kyos Featherdancing, and Janet Wallace.

Reading Dykewomon's poetry, her novels, and the issues of *Sinister Wisdom* that she published, Dykewomon's practice of building community around her is evident. She gathered writers and readers; she brought lesbians into being through her words, in the pages of *Sinister Wisdom*, and through the material practices of living her life. Speaking to Felman in 2011, Dykewomon reveals the significance of poetry in her personal cosmology. She told Felman,

> I want a world without rabbis, a world without specific holy texts. That is, I want a multiplicity of holy texts. Imagine if all that weekly energy of reading and interpreting Torah portions was poured into the poetry of Muriel Rukeyser or Irena Klepfisz or June Jordan or Chrystos—if our poets were our sources of comfort, guidance, moral values, prophecy, right conduct. It is Jewish, of course, to hold Judaism suspect.

The significance of poetry for Dykewomon is evident in this new selection of poetry from over her lifetime. *What Can I Ask* is a celebration, a cry, a song, and a story. Dykewomon's vision of intimacy among women, captured elegantly in *Fragments from Lesbos*, is a vision that enchanted me as a reader. It is a vision also expressed in all of the other elements of Dykewomon's cultural work. Dykewomon is a cultural worker, nurturing and expanding lesbians and lesbian communities.

Twenty years after Elana Dykewomon turned the editorship of *Sinister Wisdom* over to Akiba Onada-Sikwoia, it is an extraordinary pleasure for *Sinister Wisdom* to publish *What Can I Ask: Selected and New Poems* by Elana Dykewomon. The continued publication of *Sinister Wisdom* is a testament to her vision and labor over a lifetime to growing, sustaining, and nurturing lesbian communities.

I started *Sinister Wisdom's* **Sapphic Classics** series to keep collections of lesbian poetry in print and available to reach new readers. Collections of lesbian poetry fall out of print too quickly; they are not collected enough by libraries. Lesbian work is too easily forgotten, erased, rendered obsolete. Books by lesbian poets sometimes need time to find their readers—and for their readers to find them. **Sapphic Classics** return them to the world for new discovery and conscious re-engagement.

Another challenge that our most established lesbian poets face is publishing collections of selected poems. Selected—or Collected—poems signify a poet's accomplishment to larger communities of poets and literary critics. They mark a distinguished body of work, a body of work that needs and deserves serious critical attention. With this third **Sapphic Classic,** *Sinister Wisdom* addresses the dearth of selected work by lesbian poets with the release of *What Can I Ask: Selected and New Poems* of Elana Dykewomon.

In "A Fool for love," Dykewomon writes:

I want to imagine a world
in which we thrive
where difference engages us
and root holds fast with root.

Dykewomon's vision of lesbian communities in this poem expresses my modest hope for this book. I want *What Can I Ask* to be a root for Dykewomon that holds fast, binding her poetry to the roots of other righteous lesbian-feminist poets, providing a site for engaged reading and interpretation, and operating as a source of "comfort, guidance, moral values, [and] prophecy."

Julie R. Enszer
April 2015

Julie R. Enszer is the editor and publisher of *Sinister Wisdom*. She is the author of *Sisterhood* (Sibling Rivalry Press, 2013) and *Handmade Love* (A Midsummer Night's Press, 2010). She is editor of *Milk & Honey: A Celebration of Jewish Lesbian Poetry* (A Midsummer Night's Press, 2011); *Milk & Honey* was a finalist for the Lambda Literary Award in Lesbian Poetry.

Elana Dykewomon Bibliography

BOOKS

Risk, a novel, Bywater Books, Ann Arbor, MI, 2009.

Moon Creek Road, stories, Spinsters Ink, Denver, Spring 2003.

Beyond the Pale, an historical novel. Raincoast Books, Vancouver, BC, Fall 2003—reissued with a new preface (originally published by Press Gang, 1997). 1998 Lambda Literary Assoc. Award (The Lammy), Best Lesbian Novel; 1998 Publishers' Triangle Award (The Ferro-Grumley), Best Lesbian Fiction; German translation: *Sarahs Töchter*, Krug & Schadenberg, Berlin,1999; UK edition: Onlywomen Press, London, 2000. Available currently as an e-book from Open Road Media (openroadmedia.com) and as a audio-book from Audible.com

Nothing Will Be As Sweet As The Taste, selected poems. Onlywomen Press, London, August 1995.

Riverfinger Women, a novel (under Elana Nachman). Daughters, Inc., 1974; republished by Naiad Press in 1992 with a new Afterword. German trans.: *Frauen aus dem Fluss*, Amazonen Frauenverlag, West Berlin, 1977. Available currently as an e-book from Open Road Media (openroadmedia.com) and as audio-book from Audible.com

Fragments from Lesbos, poetry. Diaspora Distribution, 1981. OP

They Will Know Me By My Teeth, short stories and poetry. Megaera, 1976. OP

SELECTED NON-FICTION, ESSAYS, INTRODUCTIONS, AND ANTHOLOGIES

"Living 'anyway:' Stories of Access," essay, *Journal of Lesbian Studies*, Vol. 18(1), 2014 http://www.tandfonline.com/toc/wjls20/18/1#.U_kkHkhyHgo

"In Search of the Fabled Fat Woman," essay, *Journal of Fat Studies*, Vol. 3(1), 2014, http://www.tandfonline.com/toc/ufts20/3/1#.U_kICEhyHgo

"Who Says We're Extinct?" and "Walking on the Moon," essays in *Trivia—Voices of Feminism*, issues 10–11, http://www.triviavoices.net/index.html

"Are We Ready to Throw Our Weight Around?—Fat Women and Political Activism," *The Fat Studies Reader*, E. Rothblum & S. Solovay, eds., Univ. of California Press, Fall 2007.

"Foreword: What we have to give—" *What I Want From You*, Linda Zeiser and Trena Machado, eds., Raw Art Press, 2006.

"Lesbian Quarters: On Building Space, Identity, Institutional Memory and Resources," *Journal of Lesbian Studies*, Vol. 9(1–2), Harrington Park Press, NY, 2005.

Featured writer: www.lodestarquarterly.com, Issue 10, Summer 2004. Includes interview, poem, and a memoir, *Milk and Honey*.

"The Body Politic—Meditations on Identity," essay, *This Bridge We Call Home*, Gloria Anzaldúa & AnaLouise Keating, eds., Routledge, NY, 2002.

"Changing the World," essay, *Journal of Lesbian Studies*, Vol. 5(3), Harrington Park Press, NY, 2001.

"A Manifesto, A Genealogy, A Cause—*Found Treasures*," essay/review, *Bridges,* Vol. 5(2), Eugene, OR, 1995.

"The Ex-patriot and Her Name" (essay), *InVersions—Writing by Dykes, Queers & Lesbians,* Press Gang, Vancouver, Canada, 1991.

"The Fourth Daughter's 400 Questions" (essay), *Nice Jewish Girls—A Lesbian Anthology*, Beacon Press, 1989.

About the Author

Elana Dykewomon is a Jewish lesbian-feminist activist, award-winning author, editor, and teacher. Her first novel, *Riverfinger Women* (published in 1974), was chosen for *The Publishing Triangle's* list of *100 best lesbian and gay novels*. Dykewomon is also the author of *They Will Know Me by My Teeth: stories and poems of lesbian struggle, celebration, and survival* (1976), *Fragments from Lesbos* (1981), *Nothing Will Be As Sweet As The Taste: Selected Poems 1974-1994* (1995), *Beyond the Pale* (1998, winner of the Lambda Literary and Ferro-Grumley Awards for Best Lesbian Novel), *Moon Creek Road* (2003), and *Risk* (2009, Lambda Best Lesbian Novel short-list). She has been a regular contributor to *Bridges*, a magazine of writing by Jewish women, the periodicals *Common Lives/Lesbian Lives, Trivia* and *The Journal of Lesbian Studies.* Dykewomon's essays have been included in *InVersions: Writing by Dykes, Queers & Lesbians* (Betsy Warland and Valerie Speidel, editors, 1991), *Shadow on a Tightrope* (Lisa Schoenfielder and Barb Weiser, editors, 1995), and *This Bridge We Call Home* (Gloria Anzaldúa and AnaLouise Keating, editors, 2002). Most recently, Dykewomon was awarded the 2009 James Duggins Outstanding Mid-Career Novelist's Prize. Dykewomon currently lives in Oakland, California with her spouse, Susan Levinkind and rescue dog, Alice B. Toklas, among friends, making trouble for hierarchies whenever she can. Elana Dykewomon was the editor of *Sinister Wisdom* from 1987 to 1994.

A Midsummer Night's Press

A Midsummer Night's Press was founded by Lawrence Schimel in New Haven, CT in 1991. Using a letterpress, it published broadsides of poems by Nancy Willard, Joe Haldeman, and Jane Yolen, among others, in signed, limited editions of 126 copies, numbered 1-100 and lettered A-Z. In 1993, the publisher moved to New York and the press went on hiatus until 2007, when it began publishing perfect-bound, commercially-printed books, under the imprints:

Fabula Rasa

Fabula Rasa: devoted to works inspired by mythology, folklore, and fairy tales. Titles from this imprint include *Fairy Tales for Writers* by Lawrence Schimel, *Fortune's Lover: A Book of Tarot Poems* by Rachel Pollack, *Fairy Tales in Electri-city* by Francesca Lia Block, *The Last Selchie Child* by Jane Yolen, and *What If What's Imagined Were All True* by Roz Kaveney.

Body Language

Body Language: devoted to texts exploring questions of gender and sexual identity. Titles from this imprint include *This is What Happened in Our Other Life* by Achy Obejas, *Banalities* by Brane Mozetic (translated from the Slovene by Elizabeta Zargi with Timothy Liu), *Handmade Love* by Julie R. Esnzer, *Mute* by Raymond Luczak; *Milk and Honey: A Celebration of Jewish Lesbian Poetry* edited by Julie R. Enszer, *Dialectic of the Flesh* by Roz Kaveney, *Fortunate Light* by David Bergman, *Deleted Names* by Lawrence Schimel, *This Life Now* by Michael Broder, and *When I Was Straight* by Julie Marie Wade.

Periscope

Periscope: devoted to works of poetry in translation by women writers. The first tiles are: *One is None* by Estonian poet Kätlin Kaldmaa (translated by Miriam McIlfatrick), *Anything Could Happen* by Slovenian poet Jana Putrle (translated by Barbara Jursa), and *Dissection* by Spanish poet Care Santos (translated by Lawrence Schimel).

Sinister Wisdom

Sinister Wisdom is a multicultural lesbian literary & art journal that publishes four issues each year. Publishing since 1976, *Sinister Wisdom* works to create a multicultural, multi-class lesbian space. *Sinister Wisdom* seeks to open, consider and advance the exploration of community issues. *Sinister Wisdom* recognizes the power of language to reflect our diverse experiences and to enhance our ability to develop critical judgment, as lesbians evaluating our community and our world.

Editor and Publisher: Julie R. Enszer, PhD
Board of Directors: Cheryl Clarke, Kathleen DeBold, Julie R. Enszer, Sue Lenaerts, Susan Levinkind, Joan Nestle, Judith K. Witherow
Office Manager: Susan Levinkind

Statements made and opinions expressed in this publication do not necessarily reflect the views of the publisher, board members, or editor(s) of *Sinister Wisdom*.
SINISTER WISDOM, founded 1976
Former editors and publishers:
Harriet Ellenberger (aka Desmoines) and Catherine Nicholson (1976-1981)
Michelle Cliff and Adrienne Rich (1981-1983)
Michaele Uccella (1983-1984)
Melanie Kaye/Kantrowitz (1983-1987)
Elana Dykewomon (1987-1994)
Caryatis Cardea (1991-1994)
Akiba Onada-Sikwoia (1995-1997)
Margo Mercedes Rivera-Weiss (1997-2000)
Fran Day (2004-2010)
Julie R. Enszer & Merry Gangemi (2010-2013)
Julie R. Enszer (2013-)
Subscribe online: www.SinisterWisdom.org

Join *Sinister Wisdom* on Facebook: www.Facebook.com/SinisterWisdom

Sinister Wisdom is a U.S. non-profit organization; donations to support the work and distribution of *Sinister Wisdom* are welcome and appreciated.

Consider including *Sinister Wisdom* in your will.